WILD COOKING

Thirty years ago, Richard Mabey educated and broadened the nation's palate with his bestselling guide to edible wild plants, *Food for Free*. Now, in *Wild Cooking*, he describes how foraging can be for cooking styles as well as succulent wildings.

As the *Observer* critic writes, Richard Mabey 'conveys both delight and wisdom'. Highly praised for his poetic prose style and his challenging ideas, he is a prize-winning writer, conservationist and botanist, whose books include *Whistling in the Dark*, *The Common Ground*, *Flora Britannica*, *Nature Cure* and most recently *Beechcombings*. Brought up in the Chilterns, Richard Mabey now lives in Norfolk with his partner, Polly Munro.

'Create your own slice of the good life by getting creative in the kitchen . . . Who said the simplest things can't be the finest?'
Sunday Times

'Takes us back 30 years to when cooking was fun. Here is a man who reads, walks about with his eyes open, travels, and has the knack of enjoyment . . . it is an adventure'
Guardian

'A real pleasure to read . . . he describes the making of food with such purity and simplicity that the reader feels close to the action'
William Leith

'It's charming. Who can resist chapters on Scrumping, Gleaning and Vegetable Road Kill, or The Pig's Squeal?'
Evening Standard

'It sparkles with shared insights polished by decades of dedicated interest in ingredients, free ones ideally. It's the sort of book every member of the Guild should aspire to write, because it's a proper food book . . . Mabey is quirky, creative, celebratory'
Journal of the Guild of Food Writers

RICHARD MABEY
WITH POLLY MUNRO

Wild Cooking

Recipes, Tips and Other Improvisations
in the Kitchen

ILLUSTRATIONS BY
James Munro

VINTAGE BOOKS
London

Published by Vintage 2009

2 4 6 8 10 9 7 5 3 1

Copyright © Richard Mabey
Illustrations copyright © James Munro 2008

Richard Mabey has asserted his right under the Copyright, Designs
and Patents Act 1988 to be identified as the author of this work

First published in Great Britain in 2008 by
Chatto & Windus with the title *The Full English Cassoulet*

Vintage
Random House, 20 Vauxhall Bridge Road,
London SW1V 2SA

www.vintage-books.co.uk

Addresses for companies within The Random House Group Limited
can be found at: www.randomhouse.co.uk/offices.htm

The Random House Group Limited Reg. No. 954009

A CIP catalogue record for this book
is available from the British Library

ISBN 9780099522966

The Random House Group Limited supports The Forest
Stewardship Council (FSC), the leading international forest
certification organisation. All our titles that are printed on
Greenpeace approved FSC certified paper carry the FSC logo.
Our paper procurement policy can be found at:
www.rbooks.co.uk/environment

Mixed Sources
Product group from well-managed
forests and other controlled sources
www.fsc.org Cert no. TT-COC-2139
© 1996 Forest Stewardship Council

Printed and bound in Great Britain by
CPI Cox & Wyman, Reading RG1 8EX

In memory of our mums –
Edna Mabey and Frances Lavender,
kitchen conjurors and gentle teachers

Contents

Introduction

Spring

Summer

Autumn

Winter

Fiesta

Introduction

The butterpat and the bicycle wheel

IT WAS my first serious food experiment, churning butter on the wheel of an upturned bicycle. I was eight or nine years old, and playing savages with our neighbourhood gang in the abandoned landscape park behind our 1930s houses. It's one of those rare moments I can replay exactly. A summer's afternoon, a group of half a dozen of us camped out on a little plateau among the birch and hawthorn scrub. Potatoes baking in the ashes of a wood fire. My dad's old Hercules bike, upside down on the grass below the laurel-draped den we'd built in the trees. All the trappings of the wild life. It's a good story, which I've told, unchallenged, too many times, and I'm surprised no one has blown my cover. Churning a pot on a bicycle wheel, after all, with a maze of brakes and cables in the way, isn't as easy as pat-a-cake.

I'd searched out a jar in Mum's kitchen (a pot which may, I fear, have once contained Sandwich Spread) small enough to wedge *between* the spokes of the back wheel, and have unimpeded progress past the wheel-forks. I filled it with top-of-the-milk, screwed the cap on tight, and began to crank the pedals by hand. We took turns, and at the end of two hours' hard graft we had a minute gobbet of unsalted butter – a transformation from milk to gold that seemed as miraculous to us as if we'd used the Philosopher's Stone, not an old bike.

But why I should have wanted to produce something as difficult and cissified, as *civilised*, as butter – and I'm pretty sure it was my idea – when I should, by schoolboy lore, have been baking gudgeons in clay or experimentally chewing worms, I haven't a clue. Except that half a century on, I'm doing exactly the same kind of thing, trying to make a passable imitation of Corsican curd cheese with the help of a couple of lemons and a pair of old tights.

I've always found making-do irresistible: improvising food out of unlikely ingredients, stretching a little a long way, trying to be a clever-dick by making real chefs' tricks accessible in an ordinary kitchen. It's a kind of culinary busking, I suppose, barefoot cookery. But I'd defend it as an approach, because it's the natural style of most cooks on the planet. Not of the highly trained professionals who produce restaurant food to exquisitely honed recipes, but of the family with a glut of cooking apples to get through; the Moroccan street-cook with just a few spices and a brazier to play with; the forager, the scavenger, the hard-up house-husband or wife who needs to be a wizard with leftovers . . . All of them have developed the knack of opportunism, of seizing the moment, the whim, the ingredient in season, of *carpe diem* cooking.

This book is a homage to that tradition. It's a modest record of some of the ideas that my partner Polly and I have explored in our kitchen and garden in Norfolk. In no way is it a conventional cookbook. It isn't organised according to different courses or kinds of food. It makes no pretence at being comprehensive or even balanced in what it covers. There is nothing on breakfasts or roast joints or cakes. Potatoes are barely mentioned, and fish not at all (see page 30 for why). Much of it is idiosyncratic, a collection of recipes which we've worked out ourselves, or simply love cooking, and which fit into what might be called the house style.

This, I hope, is what holds the book together. It's not so much an orthodox recipe book as a guide to a particular approach to food, in a world where what to eat and how to cook it have become political, even moral issues. Its loosely seasonal chapters are based on a series of reflections about food-use, about seasonality, how to cope with gluts, diversity of crops, gleaning and scrumping, energy-saving cookery. The problem of waste – and how to avoid it – runs throughout the text, as it does through the whole food supply chain, from the kitchen, where 30 per cent of purchased food goes into the bin, back to the growing fields themselves, where mechanical harvesters squander huge quantities.

As I write the world is entering – not for the first time – a cereal shortage, as yields in drought-stricken grain belts begin to fall, and diets in Asia become westernised and switch from pulses to grain-raised beef. In the panic to redress these shortages there is the ominous prospect of a return to the scorched-earth, intensive agricultural practices of the 60s and 70s, with all the long-term ecological devastation they wreaked. I have a look at this arable addiction, and ask whether there might be more benign ways of providing staple carbohydrates.

The recipes that follow each essay – an entirely personal and whimsical selection – are part of the argument, small-scale practical responses to the problems. Some of them we've worked up ourselves, but most are inspired by time-honoured dishes in the vernacular traditions of Europe, North Africa and Asia. I hope the adaptations we've developed are relevant to our increasingly vulnerable eco-systems. They're based chiefly on local and seasonal ingredients, make use of surpluses, are light on energy, and relish the great variety of organic life.

But *Wild Cooking* is no austerity manual. Many of the dishes you might reasonably call buxom, and though they're based on home-grown staples, don't stint on flavourings and flourishes. Above all it's about enjoying the business of cooking, the cutting and cossetting and sampling. Anyone who has not yet tried making pickles under a brick, or stuffing morel mushrooms with a mustard spoon, is missing half the fun of feeding.

Roots, and routes

THE BICYCLE BUTTERPAT was a creation of its time. I grew up in the days of rationing that followed World War 2, and dried egg breakfasts and cheap lunches in the local British Restaurant were regular experiences. My mother's cooking – like that of so many of her contemporaries – was a cabaret of brilliant stand-up performances in the face of the grim glare of austerity. Nearly half a century on, all us four kids remember her bacon and onion suet-roll, which she regularly cooked for five people with no more than three or four rashers of bacon. Its savour still haunts me, and makes me yearn to cook it for myself again, and to be thin enough to eat it, every Thursday.

My mother didn't so much teach me about cooking, as simply invite me into the process. From a very early age I was helping to make Yorkshire puddings and pastry, learning how to get the lumps out of gravies and white sauce before you added most of the liquid; slowly picking up the skill of stringing runner beans and slicing them on the diagonal (and realising that they tasted different from beans cut straight across), and later, more sophisticated cutting disciplines, too: fine-chopping mint for sauce (and learning to use a little *hot* water on the leaves before adding the vinegar and sugar); how to remove the gristle from kidneys without ripping them to shreds, and extricate the ventricles from ox and sheep hearts. I also acquired from Mum – maybe genetically – the luckiest gift a cook can have, a kind of culinary perfect pitch, an instinctive sense of what goes with what before you've actually tried the combination. Mum astonished us once by picking a sprig from a newly planted clump of southern-wood (not used as a culinary herb in this country for three or four centuries) and including it in a bacon and veal casserole – a brilliant pairing for the sour, aniseed-and-lemon scent of the southernwood that she can only have conjured up from inside her imagination. My brother David – whose cult journal *Breadlines* (1975) recounted a kind of making-do in more stringent financial circumstances – was cooking chicken and plums back in the early 70s.

I did my own stuff in the kitchen too. I suspect my memory of being only four years old when I made my first solo chocolate cake is a fantasy. (I wanted to include every powder in the larder, and the arrowroot and custard were on the top shelf, beyond my reach. It set remarkably well, I seem to remember.) But I was good at fudge and fondants, and soon at cheese sauce and icing and mushrooms.

At home, I was really just a *sous chef*, doing accompaniments and preparations but not the real magic. I could knock up a perfect Yorkshire pudding batter, but I was never the one that slipped it under the meat and timed its exquisite efflorescence. (And I still can't make Yorkshire puddings rise and then hunker down in a juicy slab in the way Mum could.)

The Scouts helped. We had an annual cooking competition on the common on the day allotted for the school Cadet Corps to play their war games in the bracken, and I learned how to make lemon pond pudding – another teasing delicacy that dietary correctness has drummed out of most homes – in a billy-can, over a wood fire.

In my late teens I joined in the mobile dinner party game (starter at one house, main course at another, and so on . . .), and it was in trying to find ideas for this rolling pantomime that I chanced on my first real cookery book, Lesley Blanch's *Round the World in Eighty Dishes* (1962). Its blend of glamorous travel documentary and picaresque dishes was heady stuff for a stay-at-home country boy. There seemed to be no harem kitchen or gipsy doss-down anywhere in the world where Blanch hadn't wandered in and gossiped with the cooks. She had an exotic line in nicknames for dishes. 'Bandit's Joy' was named for one of her lovers, a Macedonian brigand who wore 'at least three embroidered jackets' under his sheepskin coat. Its combination of potatoes fried with honey and nutmeg was his favourite dish. 'The Zombie's Secret' was a silky confection of avocados, bananas, cream cheese and coconut from the black-magic

backwaters of Haiti. All you needed was a fork or a whisk. The ingredients – or voodoo – did the rest: 'It is said to have been made best by a poor slave, who having died, became a Zombie, and was therefore kept making it for everyone, day after day.' Cookbooks of this era are full of apocryphal stories about the origins of dishes – like the one Blanch relates about the dish that became my first party-piece, Chicken Marengo. It seems, with hindsight, appropriate that this also was a story of improvisation. 'After the Battle of Marengo, Napoleon and his staff . . . found themselves separated from their supply wagons. The one cook who was with them had nothing for supper but chickens and nothing to cook with them but tomatoes . . .'

Inventing recipes of my own began when I first discovered the north Norfolk coast and became fascinated by the local habit of eating shoreline plants – a practice which became the theme of my first book, *Food for Free* (1972), about Britain's edible plants. When it came to obscure growths such as sea-purslane and Jew's-ear fungus there was no option but fabricating my own recipes. No others existed.

Much of this early experimentation happened in the tiny galley of a converted lifeboat in Blakeney harbour – which tempted me into new layers of improvisation. I began making rashly extravagant dishes for large numbers of people in a very confined space. It often went disastrously wrong. Wild fennel was a speciality of the coast, and one evening I thought I'd have a go at Elizabeth David's recipe for that spectacular Provençal fish dish, *rouget flambé au fenouil,* in which red mullet is grilled over a bed of dried fennel stalks, and the whole lot is flambéed in brandy. I used too much brandy, a woodstack of tinder-dry fennel, and the resulting inferno – not a calming event in a space of about two square metres – turned the mullet into charcoal bricks.

Books were an influence, but more when they were about food history and techniques than straightforward recipes. Dorothy Hartley's epic *Food in England* had the deepest effect on me. Hartley was a pioneering woman journalist, an instinctive anthropologist, and she'd wandered England between the wars, recording customs and practices in ordinary houses and farms. The techniques and recipes in the book are extraordinary for their vividness and ingenuity, and have the authentic tang of the home kitchen. I sensed her spirit years later in books by Nigel Slater, Jamie Oliver and Sam and Sam Clark – all cooks who love hunting down back-street vernacular dishes, have no truck with rigid recipes, and love using their *hands* as utensils – even on TV. The hand – as measurer, stirrer, poker, sampler – is the signature tool of the barefoot cook.

But watching cooks – just as I'd watched my mother – and trying to work out what was in their dishes influenced me more than any book. The turning-point was my first trip to the Mediterranean. I was about twenty, and studying politics and philosophy at Oxford.

One long vacation a small gang of us motored down through France, heading for the Pyrenees and a friend's villa inland from Gerona. Paris was baking, with temperatures in the mid-90s, and I remember experiencing, for the first time in my life, the exquisite pain of being unquenchably thirsty.

Our host took us down to an Arab quarter near St Michel. The North African chefs were working outside, sizzling meatballs over charcoal and gas stoves. I leaned on a railing, an immense bottle of orangeade in my hand, gawping at it all as if it were some kind of street entertainment, a show by busking fire-eaters and jugglers. *Al fresco* cooking was barely known in Britain then, certainly not in restaurants. One chef in particular caught my eye. He was frying green peppers in a large, shallow pan, with what looked like small sausages. He added handfuls of tomatoes and pounded them until they were puréed. Then, with a theatrical flourish, he broke half a dozen eggs on to the bubbling surface. They set, and this was the dish he sent to the table. It was the cleverest and strangest combination I had ever seen. But I never got to eat it. I don't think I even gathered its name (*chakchouka*) before we went off to a restaurant to eat a more humdrum meal of carrot *rapée* and *bifstek*.

But a memory of how it was made – a vision of eggs floating in a southern mix of spicy reds and greens – went with me down to Spain. We were based in a villa on a hillside at Palamos, overlooking the sea. The house was ringed with pine trees, and at the top of the hill we imagined we could see mirages of the North African coast. We ate paellas endlessly, in tiny beach cafés under ragged parasols, where the cooks stirred pans as big as dustbin-lids on braziers set in the sand. The experience of those lunches has stayed with me, and every time I use saffron in cooking I can recall every sensual detail: the scents of cooked shellfish and Ambre Solaire, the feel of warm salt drying on the skin, the chutzpah of the waiter who teased us for not eating soft-shell crabs whole, then grabbed them from our plates and ate them himself.

One afternoon, out for a drive along the thready roads inland, we came up against a broken-down lorry. It was full of water-melons. There was no way past, and the spirit of *mañana* soon fell upon us. We chatted with the driver as best we could, watching a farmer, dressed in nothing except a transparent polythene bag, driving about his field on a small tractor. When the lorry was eventually mended, its driver made his apologies with a gift of melons. I had the feast planned by the time we got back to the villa. Make the melons into soup with some smoky local *jamón,* and follow up with a *chakchouka* reconstructed from memory. It worked, surprisingly, given that I'd never attempted anything remotely like it before. We ate it lounging on a floor strewn with pine fronds, like decadent Berbers, and washed it down with dirt-cheap Spanish champagne.

Here, by way of introduction to the amateur art of making-do, are the recipes, modified slightly by later experience (for notes on measures, see page 32).

Melon and ham soup

FOR 2 PEOPLE

1 large water-melon, or 2 smaller honeydews
1 ham hock or knuckle, or about 250g smoked Spanish ham
1 orange

Cut the melons in half, scoop out the seeds and discard, then cut and spoon the flesh out into a saucepan. Add the ham, and simmer for about half an hour. The melon should generate enough liquid on its own, so don't add any extra water unless you prefer a really thin soup. Remove the ham, liquidise the liquor if you wish, or leave the scraps of melon pulp to float about, and serve warm (not hot), with thin slices of orange floating on the top.

Chakchouka

FOR 2 PEOPLE

2 small onions
sunflower oil
4 cloves of garlic
1 whole red chilli
2 large sweet peppers, red and green
spicy sausages (about 250g)
500g of tomatoes (fresh or tinned)
2 to 4 free-range eggs

Slice the onions thinly and fry in a good slug of sunflower oil until they are golden. Add the garlic, crushed and roughly chopped, and the thinly sliced chilli, having scraped out the seeds if you don't want too hot a dish. Cook gently for a further 2 minutes. Prepare the sweet peppers by quartering, cutting out the inner ribs, and then slicing into strips about 2cm wide. Slice the sausages into 3cm lengths. Small Moroccan *merguez* are the best and most authentic, but if you can't get hold of these, use any spicy chipolata, or *chorizo* sliced 1cm thick. Add both ingredients to the pan and sauté until the peppers begin to soften and the sausages are slightly browned – 10 minutes at the maximum.

Meanwhile, if using fresh tomatoes, pour boiling water on them in a separate bowl, leave for a few minutes, then remove the skins under a cold tap. Halve them and add them to the stew, with a little seasoning if you wish. Simmer for a further 10 minutes, stirring and pressing with a wooden spoon, until the tomatoes are well puréed and some of their water has boiled off. Finally break the eggs – 1 or 2 per person – on top of the stew while it's still simmering, and cook till they are just set. Alternatively, you can beat the eggs first and stir them in to the mixture, scrambling them in effect. Serve hot.

Kumquats in syrup
FOR 2 PEOPLE

I'm hazy about what we had for sweet that evening. Probably peaches and more oranges. Sharp and sweet is what you want after a *chakchouka*. There is a Moorish tradition of preparing citrus fruits in syrup as a dessert. Small tangerines served this way were a classic Iraqi dish. I've given a recipe which uses that neglected fruit the kumquat, one of the few citrus fruits where the thin peel can be eaten whole, even when uncooked. Kumquats came originally from China, moving west to Spain along Islamic trading and military routes, and it was in a market in Gerona that summer that I first saw them. They are slightly acid, but the large amount of sugar needed for concentrating into the syrup will deal with that. You can leave a good deal of the syrup in the pan.

500g sugar

250ml water

a squeeze of lemon juice

20 kumquats

Put the sugar, water and lemon juice into a saucepan, replace the lid and bring to the boil. Add the kumquats – simply cut in half, nothing more – and simmer for an hour, until they are soft. Lift out the fruit and arrange on a dish. Reduce the syrup by simmering further, until it is just thick enough to stick slightly to the spoon. Pour a little over the kumquat halves.

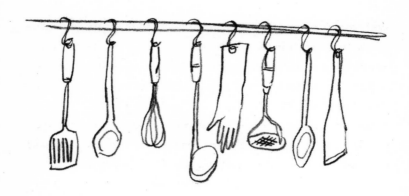

Equipment and provisions

Knives out

THE ONLY indispensable equipment for the recipes that follow is a good set of knives. Clever cutting can transform over-familiar ingredients into new taste-and-texture experiences – as Mum well knew. I reckon four types of knife are essential: a heavy chopper, with a blade about 10 x 20cm, for quartering chickens, slicing vegetables, chopping herbs, squashing garlic. A longer, narrower blade, about 5 x 30cm, for more intricate work on vegetables. A filleting knife, with a thin and tapering blade, for boning fish and meat. And a short, sharp dagger, for fiddly tasks like peeling apples and slivers of skin from oranges, taking the eyes out of potatoes, etc.

Good potato peelers, especially the type in which the blade is set in a triangle at right angles to the shaft – rather in the manner of a safety razor – are invaluable, and will skin everything from lemons to marrows in double-quick time.

Pots

At the very least, have one good casserole dish, to take about 3 litres. One large shallow non-stick frying pan, preferably with an optional lid. A set of steamers in a deep saucepan. A good-sized wok.

Desert Island flavourings

On a later trip to France, exploring the Languedoc hills with my old friend Richard Simon, we chanced on a tiny *routier* in the village of Saissac. We were the only foreigners there, and the place was encouragingly full of blue-overalled truckers. There was no menu, no ordering, nor, it seemed, anything resembling a vegetable. We just sat there and the heroic food arrived. It consisted almost entirely of immense platefuls of protein: charcuterie, old cockerel (cooked with prunes), local cheeses. When the chicken was served, the driver sitting next to me fished in his pocket and pulled out something resembling an angler's fly-box. It was divided into nine compartments, and in each one was a small heap of herbs. My French wasn't good enough then to understand what all their names meant, but I could recognise thyme and peppercorns and nutmeg.

I like the idea of a culinary emergency kit, with which you can administer first-aid to away-from-home meals. It might not go down well in a Gordon Ramsay restaurant, and certainly not at a private dinner party. But even as a mental exercise, it helps bring into focus what are the transforming flavourings most useful in a kitchen.

This is a list Polly and I drew up of our essentials, the ingredients with which you can transform any intrinsically bland dish or over-familiar staple into something new and interesting. This is not, of course, a comprehensive list of what flavourings you need in the larder. It's simply the kit we'd take with us for our *Desert Island Discs* luxury item.

GARLIC Indispensable. The violet variety is strongest.

LEMONS A wonderful sharpening condiment for steak, soups, stews, desserts.

BLACK KALAMATA OLIVES Wrinkly and tangy, and free of that stretched plastic feel of brine-pickled inferior varieties. Good to add to cooked meat dishes as well as salads.

EXTRA VIRGIN OLIVE OIL Preferably two sorts, a heavier one for cooking and a lighter, spicier one for dressings. If you can get hold of them, experiment with oils from unconventional sources. Australian, Californian and Tunisian oils can be spectacular, good enough to drink from the bottle.

SOY SAUCE Has been in Britain since the eighteenth century, and is a useful deepener of texture in soups and meat dishes, as well as Oriental recipes.

CUMIN SEED Quintessential ingredient of Middle Eastern cooking. Good with cooked fruit, too.

FRESH CHILLIES Much more flavoursome than the dried powder. Available now in all kinds of strengths, so test and find your acceptable level. Remove seeds and pith to cool them down.

ROOT GINGER Again, incomparably more aromatic than the dried powder. Essential for many Chinese and Indian dishes. Buy in small quantities at a time, as it dries out once cut.

SHERRY VINEGAR To my mind the most flexible of vinegars, for its combination of richness and acidity.

HERBS The most adaptable is thyme, either dried or fresh, which can be used in just about any dish – meat, fish, salad, veg. Also fresh chives, fresh parsley, fresh mint and fresh coriander leaves. (Len Deighton's recommendation for coriander: 'Throw it into any open pot.')

Sources

Organic

THIS, STRICTLY, MEANS food grown without the help of artifical chemicals (fertilisers, pesticides), though many products on the market interpret it more liberally, as food grown with *fewer* chemicals. Take it as read that, wherever it's available and affordable, organic produce is preferable. I am not totally convinced that organic always tastes better (freshness is a better predictor of this in my experience) but the other arguments for it are irrefutable.

- Chemical farming has devastated plant and insect life on the planet. That is what it is intended to do. The reverberations have spread right up the food chain. Even if you don't believe this is ethically wrong in itself, reflect on the fact that the pollinating and predatory insects so essential to balanced farming systems have suffered just as much as so-called pests.
- Chemical farming is carbon heavy. Most pesticides and herbicides are

made from oil-based hydrocarbons, and their production produces immense amounts of CO_2. This will quite soon be its downfall, as rising oil prices make the cost of farm chemicals prohibitive. The wild card is GM technology, which may – at a so far unquantifiable ecological price – reduce the costs of intensive, chemical farming.

• But remember *all* cultivation of the soil is inimical to wildlife (and carbon heavy). That is what it is meant to do – replace complicated wild ecosystems of the forest with simplified man-made ones. Produce from 'farmed forests' (see page 113), orchards, etc., does at least preserve some kind of ecosystem.

Local

Wherever you can, buy food which is grown close to you. It's fresher, supports local economies, and its transport has a low carbon footprint. Haunt farm gate shops, farmers' markets, independent green-grocers, and beat the supermarkets by by-passing them. (This also goes for producers, who have too willingly become the food combines' poodles.) But don't be dogmatic about food miles. Tomatoes grown in the Mediterranean sun and flown to Britain have a smaller carbon impact than tomatoes grown locally in heated greenhouses. Potatoes grown in infertile soils in Kenya, say, and then flown to the UK may be responsible for fewer total carbon emissions than potatoes grown locally in fertile carbon-rich soils.

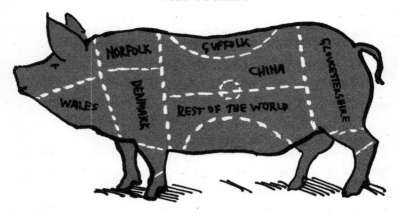

Meat

If you can't always buy organic pork, lamb, beef, chickens, eggs, etc., go for free-range, local suppliers, and outlets that specify how they are treating their animals. Support rare breeds to help sustain genetic diversity. But meat production is the costliest way (in all senses) of producing food on most land, and meat products play a secondary role to vegetables in this book.

Fish

Despite their health-giving properties, and their sheer delight as taste experiences, I've not included fish in this book, beyond the odd portion of prawns. I'm pessimistic about whether wild fish populations are sustainable in the face of intensive factory trawling, and fish farming has so far proved difficult to sustain without heavy use of pesticides and antibiotics. The best way of conserving the planet's fish seems to me to eat as few of them as possible.

Wild vegetables and fruit

I've tried to avoid going over the same ground as *Food for Free,* though there are new thoughts, for example, on spring greens and wilding plums and apples. But this isn't an identification guide. If you are unsure about the identification of any wild food in the book, go to one of the field-guides listed in the reference section at the back.

Seasoning

If kitchen busking is partly about seizing the moment, the moment which must be most enthusiastically seized is, of course, the season. A calendar season, a vegetable in season, the moment – sometimes only a single day – when a fruit is perfectly seasoned, immaculately ripe. The old Suffolk smallholder who grows asparagus near us in the sandy soils of the Waveney Valley understands this perfectly. Towards the end of April notices go up in the lanes around his property announcing: 'Asparagus SOON.' The word goes round the district as smartly as a tray of canapés, and the idea of ruining that exquisite anticipation by buying *foreign* sparrow-grass in those waiting days would not sully anyone's mind.

Seasonality is ideally about the matching of moment with mood. To have strawberries available every day of the year – flown in expensively from California or Spain – devalues not only the fruit itself but the specialness of the occasion on which it's enjoyed. If air-freighted fruit is profligate with carbon, it's also profligate with the human spirit, levelling and dumbing down the experiences of eating.

A note on recipes, quantities, etc.

M OST OF THE RECIPES below are for two people, though some of the more robust dishes are for four. But the *proportions* of the ingredients are more relaxed. Vernacular cooking isn't usually a matter of precise quantification. If a quantity isn't mentioned, it isn't important. Be idiosyncratic. If you don't like garlic or chilli, for instance, simply use less. Where quantities are important – e.g., in setting gelatine, or raising bread dough – they are spelt out. The golden rule if you're anxious about free-range cooking is to taste, taste, and taste again as you go along.

The book is arranged in four seasonal chapters, though this is for conceptual rather than practical reasons. Many of the dishes can be made at any time of the year.

Spring

New shoots, soft tissues, young animals. Think April breezes,
and explore the gentle art of steaming to deal with these fragile
materials. Wild greens and wild flowers are out long before garden
produce. Get a good field-guide (see pages 217–18) and go foraging.

*

T HE MOST EXTRAORDINARY spring meal I have ever eaten –
in fact it was a meal for all seasons, crammed into one
surreal evening – was cooked for me by the travel writer
Sarah Hobson. In the early 70s we'd both published our first books.
Sarah had written *Through Persia in Disguise*, about her adventures
travelling as a faux-transvestite in the male redoubts of Iran. And I'd
had a shot at introducing the arcane mysteries of eating weeds to the
convenience-eating British in *Food for Free*. Two odd rites of passage.
As is the way of things our respective eccentricities tracked each
other down. We swapped books and found ourselves making friends.

But my hedgerow foragings were small beer by the side of Sarah's
exploits. In her teenage years she'd run wild on the Scottish moors
armed with a .22 rifle. Her trip to Persia was made when she was

twenty-two. She was making belts and was fascinated by Moorish culture, and wanted to see for herself the impenetrable male enclaves of Isfahan. She cut her hair short, flattened her bosom with tight bandages, put on loose clothes and pottered about on a hired moped called Mephistopheles. I was pleased that she wasn't wearing the disguise (which had in any case looked quite unconvincing in her book-jacket photograph) when I first visited her cottage in Northamptonshire. It was early February and the meal she'd cooked for me was like her book – full of jokes and Middle Eastern grace notes, but with little botanical courtesies added for my sake.

It began with a Four Seasons starter:

WINTER: A brown hard-boiled egg, baked in its shell in a mixture of oil and Turkish coffee.

SPRING: Snowdrop buds opening in a small bowl of hot apple and cabbage soup.

SUMMER: Tiny cucumber and Marmite sandwiches served in toy plastic deckchairs.

AUTUMN: Prawns fried in turmeric and mace, with big black olives.

The eggs had been cooked for long enough to be dyed brown by the coffee, which had permeated their shell, much as saffron does when cooked with eggs in their shells.

The snowdrops, I had to tell her, were dodgy, toxic and apt to over-stimulate the heart (not a good idea on first meeting). But the sight of the buds opening limply as they bathed in the warm soup reminded me of a fantastical Persian dish I'd once read about, where nearly-opened rosebuds were served at table in a dish of hot oil.

The cucumber sandwiches were perfectly decrusted, Savoy style, and served on little striped chairs no bigger than matchboxes.

By autumn I think Sarah's imagination had waned a little, and the prawns, spices and olives were simply a strong statement of autumn colours.

This baroque array of starters was followed by a carpet-bag steak, cut open and filled with three different mustards, wrapped in herbs, hung up in her cottage's copious chimney to cook in wood smoke, and served with bulb fennel cooked with its own chopped leaves as a herb. The result was as smoky as biltong, but wonderfully succulent. The herbs seemed to have kept the meat's juices in, so that it effectively steamed itself.

A touch of the vapours

COOKING THINGS in vapour of some sort is common across the Middle East, especially with meat. Steam deals equally gently with ethereally flavoured young leaves and tender meat, and plays more of a part in cooking than is sometimes realised. There is, for instance, a Persian technique called *sofrito* (comparable with the Italian

soffrito, meaning a slowly sautéed mixture of celery, carrot and onion used as a basis of sauces). *Sofrito* is the very slow braising of meat or vegetables in a minimum of oil and water, inside a closed pot. Sometimes the pot is sealed with a ring of dough. *Sofrito* is close to our own pot-roasting, which relies more on the action of steam and vaporised meat juices than on the direct heat of the stove. I use a hybrid method, with metal foil to wrap the meat as well as seal the pot. I first tried it in the galley of a narrowboat, when a group of us were exploring the Abergavenny canal in the 1970s, and taking in the prodigious Breconshire ciders. We'd bought some mountain spring lamb and a few vegetables, and gathered bunches of wild thyme on the Brecon Beacons. We wrapped the lot in foil, and cooked the parcel in a pot for a whole afternoon in the boat's minuscule oven, while we were in a towpath pub on ciderous business.

Below is a more sophisticated version, which attempts to minimise water loss from the meat so that it's essentially cooked at steam temperature in its own juices.

Lamb steamed with thyme

FOR 4 PEOPLE

leg of lamb, 1.5 to 2kg
6 cloves of garlic
olive oil
sea salt
2 handfuls of fresh thyme

Trim the fat from the lamb, and cut away a few areas of the tough skin to expose the flesh. With a pointed knife make a dozen or so incisions 2cm deep in the flesh, and push half a clove of peeled garlic into each. Rub the lamb with olive oil and sea salt, and pack swaths of thyme around it. Encase the whole lot in several layers of kitchen foil, until you have quite a tight parcel. Put this into a casserole dish, with a centimetre or so of water. Over the open pot stretch another layer of foil so that it's held on by the lid. Cook in a slow oven for 2½ to 3 hours, checking the water level in the pot every hour, and topping up if necessary (this ensures that the lamb never gets above steam-heat).

The meat should be almost falling off the bone, and be scented with the thyme right through.

It's possible to substitute rosemary for thyme in this recipe, but it can make the meat a little bitter.

Serve with a sharp salad of spring leaves, such as the splendid over-wintering Pallo Rosso. And with a mixture of two old hippie dishes from the same decade: brown rice and lentils, better together than apart.

Rice and lentil hash

FOR 4 PEOPLE

1 cup of brown basmati rice

1 cup of red lentils (or red and green mixed)

olive oil

2 onions

Everybody has their own patent method with rice. Mine is far from original, but has the advantage of involving no washing or straining, and having been – so far – completely infallible. It involves using the proportions of one and a quarter cups of water (or one and a half with European rices, like Arborio, Calasparra, etc.) to every cup of rice. Simply bring the rice and water to the boil, cover, and simmer for 25 minutes. Turn the heat off and leave for 5 minutes. The rice should be fluffy and the grains separate without any extra attention.

Rinse the lentils in cold water, drain, and put into a saucepan with double the quantity of water. Bring to the boil, and simmer for 15 minutes. At this point the lentils will still be slightly firm to the bite. Drain and combine with the rice.

In an open pan warm 2 or 3 tablespoons of olive oil, and fry the finely chopped onions for about 10 minutes. Add the rice-lentil mixture – and anything else that takes your fancy: cubes of feta cheese, sultanas, chopped peppers, peas – and cook till the whole mixture is hot.

PS: If you want a rice and lentil dish as interesting as the main course, elaborate this into a version of the Egyptian *kosheri*. Cook the lentils as above, but use the *chilau* method (below) of cooking the rice, adding a pinch of nutmeg and a teaspoon of cinnamon during the butter-frying stage.

Chilau steamed rice

Rice too can be made silkier and nuttier by steaming. This is an Iranian method. Put the rice into a sieve and rinse with hot water. Transfer to a bowl of cold water, stir in a tablespoon of salt and allow to soak for as long as you've got. Overnight is best, but a couple of hours will do. Then drain, rinse well with cold water, and add to a panful of boiling water to which another tablespoon of salt has been added. (The salt helps the grains of rice keep separate, and is all washed out with the water eventually.) Boil for 5 or 6 minutes. Drain and rinse with lukewarm water to remove the salt.

Now comes the steaming stage. Melt 2 tablespoons of butter (or olive oil) in a pan with 2 tablespoons of water. Add the rice, and stir well until all the grains have slightly changed colour from the butter coating. Stretch a clean cloth over the pan, close it with the lid, and fold the corners of the cloth up to prevent them burning on the stove. The cloth catches and absorbs the steam as it rises from the rice, keeping the whole interior of the pot humid but not water-logged – which ensures light and well-separated grains. Steam on a low heat on top of the stove for 20 minutes.

The rice at the bottom of the pan will have been crisped and caramelised. It's considered a delicacy, known as *dig*, and is often scraped from the pan and served separately from the rice – exactly as the burnt bits are from from English milk puddings a thousand miles away.

Sweet chicken with candied oranges (Shirini polo)

FOR 2 PEOPLE

This is a recipe which uses *chilau* rice, and is adapted from an original by Claudia Roden. It's ideal for early spring, when bitter Seville oranges are still around.

250g basmati rice
20 threads of saffron
about 50g Seville orange peel
sugar
free-range chicken legs or breasts (at least 250g)
salt and pepper
butter

Prepare the rice according to the first two stages of the *chilau* method on page 39 (washing and quick boiling, with the addition of 10 threads of saffron to the water), but do not steam yet.

To prepare the candied orange peel, slice the peel from the oranges very thinly with a sharp knife or peeler, taking care not to remove any pith as well. Weigh the pieces, add the same weight of sugar, and cook in a small pan with a little water until the strips of peel are soft and sweet, and the water reduced to a syrup.

Simmer the chicken legs or breasts with enough water to cover, plus the other 10 threads of saffron, and salt and pepper. After 40 minutes remove the chicken from the pan, cut the cooked flesh from the bones, and slice into bite-sized pieces. Return it to the liquid in the pan, add the peel and its syrup, and simmer for a further 10 minutes.

Now melt a tablespoon of butter (more commonly used than oil in Middle Eastern cooking) in a heavy-bottomed saucepan or casserole dish. Put a third of the rice into the molten butter. Then build up alternate layers of rice and the chicken-peel mixture (liquid included), ending with a layer of rice.

Stretch a clean cloth over the pan, put the lid on firmly, and steam over a very low heat for 30 minutes. By this time the bitter-sweet chicken sauce will have permeated the rice. The cloth absorbs the steam, and the relative lack of condensed water dripping back on to the rice helps to keep it fluffy.

Sproutings

'SPRING', in the patois of woodmanship, is the word for the new shoots of coppiced trees, as well as for the season they sprout in – a nice elision of the whole season with its new shoots.

The sproutings of new plants – especially those that spring straight from the seed – contain more nutrients, weight for weight, than any other food product. They need to, to give the seedling a start before it has enough leaves to manufacture its own food. The original sprouted seeds were tray-grown mustard and cress, which we used to have in sandwiches with mashed hard-boiled egg. Mustard and cress were grown in peat, but you can generate sprouts hydroponically, using water as the medium instead of soil. Use a commercial sprouter, with transparent plastic trays, or sheets of damp paper in a tray.

First, soak the seeds in water for twelve hours. Then spread them out in a single layer on the tray or damp paper. Keep the tray in a well-lit, warm place, and sprinkle with lukewarm water twice a day. The sprouts should start growing in three or four days, and will consist of a small pair of leaflets (the dicotyledon) on a stalk, which will become long and leggy as the seedling searches for light. For maximum taste and crunchiness they're best harvested, using a pair of scissors, before the leaflets start to expand.

The best seeds for sprouting are those from the pea family, which are large and fast-growing. Mung beans, alfalfa, chickpeas are popular. Also some cabbage family members, such as linseed and radish. But the technique works with some garden weed seeds too. Try it with annuals such as hairy bittercress, sow-thistle, fat hen, clover, chickweed, wild radish, and harvest the seeds in

late summer. But be patient. All these species have comparatively small seeds, and will take longer to shoot and grow more slowly than the bigger pea-family fruits.

*

The forced sprouting of seeds isn't a fashionable new invention by the health-conscious. Early writers were on to the trick, though they were sometimes carried away by their own cleverness. The diarist John Evelyn, whose waspish book *Acetaria* (1699) is the earliest English treatise on salads, passes on an anecdote from a correspondent, who'd apparently invented the first chemical-free fast food, and: 'having some Friends to Dine with him, and wanting an early Salett, before they sate down to table, sowed Lettuce and some other Seeds in a certain Composition of Mould he had prepared; which within the space of two Hours, being risen near two Inches high, presented them with a delicate and tender Sallett; and this without making use of any nauseous or fulsome Mixture'.

More than a century earlier, Thomas Hill had given instructions for a slower-growing, if more plausible, mixed salad in *The Gardener's Labyrinth* (1557). From some classical gardening texts he'd gleaned the idea of 'mixed leaves' as a feature not just of the salad bowl, but of the growing plants themselves:

> If the Gardiner desire to have a plant to growe of a
> marvellous form and divers in tast, he shall with an easie

cost and light travaile perform the same, if he will properly make a hole into a round pellet made of Goats dung [Hill calls these 'terdiles'], and into the same put of the Lettice, Cresses, Basill, Rocket, and Radish seeds, and that ball wrapped in dung, be bestowed in a well laboured earth . . . and this often and gently (or by little and little) springled with water: for the radish shooting down performeth the root, but the other seeds into a height, the Lettice rising withall, and each yeelding the plant in their proper tast.

We tried this one spring. Not having access to goat dung, we made our terdiles out of horse manure, and drilled in a mixture of various lettuces, rockets and radish. They came through, but not quite in the tastefully entwined sheaf Hill seemed to promise. The dung was plainly too rich, the seeds too numerous, the different species programmed to grow at very different rates. Just a few of the more nitrogen-hungry lettuces made it, but they were well ready for picking by the time the first leaflets of radish and rocket pushed through.

A mess of greens

ON CRETE, in the early spring, large numbers of people go out into the countryside to gather *stamnagathi* (spiny chicory, *Cichorium spinosum*). The tufts of young leaves are believed to be good for the liver, a tonic and purifer after the rigours of winter. At Eastertime, on the Omalos plateau, I've seen whole families decamping from their cars in their Easter best and spending hours crouched down, digging up the young plants with a special miniature hoe. Curiously, the *stamnagathi* are usually served boiled, though in my opinion they are much tastier raw.

In the Languedoc in south-west France, spring means the gathering of wild leeks and dandelion. In the Pyrenees they make a local delicacy called *rapunzous* (patois for *repousse*) from the tips of black bryony, cooked and mashed up with hard-boiled egg and vinaigrette. In Italy and Spain, men on scooters buzz home with bunches of thin wild asparagus tied to their pannier-racks. In the American South and the Appalachians, they harvest the green called poke salad. Elvis grew up with it. Across much of the northern hemisphere, gathering wild spring greens is an essential ritual celebration, a way of putting the stodginess of the dark days to rout.

In Britain, it happened occasionally too, though usually with less gusto and a heavy dose of northern European puritanism. Before the easy availability of citrus fruit in the mid-nineteenth century, there were fads for gathering scurvy-grass and making it into early morn-ing health drinks. I've tried this and it is somewhat more rigorous than a fruit smoothie.

We should copy the continentals and start a tradition here. By March large numbers of wild plants have their young leaves showing well. Use a reliable identification book, and make a mess of greens to your own formula. Good components are:

The flowers and young leaves of white and red DEAD-NETTLE.

The flowerbuds – like yellowish broccoli – of escaped OIL-SEED RAPE, which has become an aggressive invader of road verges, and the similar buds of ALEXANDERS.

The first leaves of JACK-BY-THE HEDGE, for its slight garlic savour, and RAMSONS (see overleaf) for an even stronger garlic note.

SORREL, for its lemony sourness.

COMFREY (when it's no more than 10cm high) for cucumbery succulence.

BITTER-CRESS or LADY'S-SMOCK for pepperiness; DANDELION for bitterness; even very young DOCK, for body.

For a wild spring salad, pick and mix the leaves so that no one flavour dominates. Keep the dressing sweet and simple, as there should be enough sharp and garlicky notes already. Hazelnut oil, if you can find it, is light and makes a good base. Otherwise use sunflower oil, with just a little salt and sugar, and a dash of soy sauce beaten in.

If you want to cook the greens, use the same plants. You can also add young nettle tops, whose sting is taken away by heat, and hop shoots.

A warm mess of spring greens

Heat some oil – walnut, hazel or sunflower – in a deep pan or wok, and fry a finely chopped onion in it for 5 minutes. Add the leaves, and toss in the hot oil for no more than 1 or 2 minutes, until the sorrel has changed colour to soft brown and the other leaves are beginning to wilt. Add a sprinkle of salt and soy sauce towards the end.

Ramsons

Ramsons, our native wild garlic, is one of the most versatile of spring greens. Use the leaves until mid-May (they begin to yellow and die back after that) and, later, the little bulblets formed where the flowers have been. When I introduced the manager of a local Italian restaurant to our native garlic, he responded by adding a flurry of Tuscan improvisations to his menu: ramsons leaves torn and added, instead of basil, to a tomato sauce for pasta; various ramsons salads; and, best of all, olive oil in which the leaves had been steeped for a month, for using on sun-dried tomatoes.

Dandelion salad

Dandelion, despite a certain bitterness and a reputation immortalised in the popular name 'piss-a-bed' (in French *pissenlit*), is now sufficiently redeemed to appear in gastro-pub salads. This is an elaborate recipe from Henri Toulouse-Lautrec's cook book, *The Art of Cuisine* (c. 1890). Lautrec was a gourmand who gave extravagant dinner parties, doing much of the cooking himself, and painting his own menu cards. His book is full of barbaric ways with herons and small mammals ('having killed some marmots sunning themselves belly up in the sun with their noses in the air one sunrise in September') but I don't think I have it in my heart to boycott it a century on. (Incidentally Lautrec was also one for carrying portable seasoning, in the shape of a nutmeg and grater, which he used to flavour his port.)

'In the fields at the end of January or February, after a thaw, pick some dandelions which are beginning to grow – whose hearts already show signs of yellow.

'Wash them and dry them carefully in a cloth. Into a salad bowl put some fine olive oil or fresh walnut oil, let the salt dissolve in it, add some wine vinegar, pepper, and a small spoonful of mustard. Mix it well; crush three or four hard-boiled eggs, finely chopped, and proceed so that the whole mixture is sufficiently seasoned to taste.

'Throw in the dandelions and work them for a fairly long time into the sauce. When you are just about to serve, add and toss in a plateful of cubes of *bacon,* slightly browned and well crisped in butter, and small pieces of red herring.'

There are good ideas here. January or February are really too early for the British climate, but by March you can certainly pick new leaves, together with the yellowing hearts, by using a penknife and cutting deep into the plant, almost to the top of the root. You could omit the crushed eggs, which to my mind would make too heavy a sauce and overpower the thin leaves. But fried bacon cubes (and maybe some croutons as well) are perfect additions, the bitterness of the dandelion contrasting with the bacon's fattiness. The mixture of oil and bacon fat which remains from the frying is the best base for the dressing too – mixed, as Lautrec suggests, with wine vinegar, pepper and a smidgeon of mustard.

Broad bean hummus

This idea, which I first came across in a country pub in Suffolk, makes an unusual spring starter – though to tell the truth, it's just as good as an autumn dish with frozen broad beans, which are one of the few vegetables that endure freezing without any loss of texture or taste. In spring it needs willpower and a surplus of new broad beans to do anything other than eat them by themselves on a white plate.

500g broad beans
juice of 1 lemon
2 tablespoons olive oil
3 cloves of garlic
1 tablespoon melted butter or tahini

Blanch the broad beans in boiling water, no more than 2 minutes if they are young, maybe 3 or 4 for older tougher beans. Put into a food processor with the lemon juice, olive oil, garlic, and – if you like the nutty taste of tahini (roast sesame seed paste), which is used in conventional hummus – add a tablespoon of this. Alternatively a tablespoon of melted butter, to give a firmer, more pâté-like finish. Three 4-second bursts should be plenty. The end product should still be beany, with shards of skin and a grainy consistency.

PS: Try making hummus with *sprouted* peas or beans. The green sproutings add an exhilarating fresh nuttiness to the taste.

Eggs, shoots and leaves

IN THE MEDITERRANEAN young greens and herbs are often cooked with eggs. They're texturally supportive and not overpoweringly flavoured, and make good vehicles for the sharp colours and flavours of new shoots. The Italian *frittata* is a kind of solid omelette; the Spanish *revuelto*, an egg scramble.

Wild asparagus frittata

A dish for cooking on a southern holiday. Don't look for wild asparagus shooting up like cultivated spears straight from the ground. It winds it way through scrub and hedges, and often the tips – the top 20 to 30cm you pick – are at waist level.

Blanch the asparagus by plunging into boiling water for 2 or 3 minutes. Remove and chop into 5cm lengths. Melt a spoonful of butter in a heavy-bottomed frying pan and add beaten eggs – 2 for each person – and a dozen or so shoots of wild asparagus. *Frittata* is solider than a French-style omelette, so simply cook without stirring for about 2 or 3 minutes, until the eggs are set. Then flip the *frittata*, or turn over with a spatula, and brown the other side, or put it under the grill for another couple of minutes.

Sorrel revuelto

Revueltos, cooked more quickly and served moist, are best for thinner and more succulent greens. Sorrel and ramsons are ideal.

Beat the eggs – 2 per person – in a bowl with a little salt. (Always beat eggs for omelettes and scrambling very lightly, some way short of frothing, otherwise they become puddingy when cooked.) Warm a little olive oil in a pan and add the chopped leaves. Fry gently until they begin to darken and turn soft. Add the beaten eggs, and stir with the leaves until they have set to the consistency you like. This will only take a minute or so.

Flower cooking

IN 1932, Florence White, founder of the English Folk Cookery Association, published a book entitled *Good Things in England: A Practical Cookery Book for Everyday Use*. It was a precocious idea. She wanted to produce an indigenous food archive, and she set about the job by inviting non-professional cooks to contribute their personal, or parish, recipes for classic English dishes. (They were chiefly country housewives, but included the odd judge and cleric – and one monstrous conceit from Boodle's Club, for grouse stuffed with bananas.) She wasn't able to repeat the formula when she published *Flowers as Food* two years later. Flowers, except for a few perennial favourites like dandelion and cowslip (both for wine), were no longer common kitchen currency, and Mrs White was confined, this time, to using book recipes going back as far as the hey-day of flower cookery in the Elizabethan period.

It took more than half a century for the idea of cooking with flowers to become fashionable again – ironically at just the moment when it became *un*fashionable to advocate their mass picking, because of the possible impact on wild flower populations. (Mrs White gives no less than fifteen recipes for cowslips, one of them for cowslip syrup, which specifies one whole pound of the freshly gathered blossoms.) Fortunately there are plenty of garden flowers which can be used. And a sense of proportion is beginning to soften the political correctness that frowned on all wild-flower picking in the late twentieth century: harvesting dandelions, or a few about-to-fall petals from a wild rose, simply isn't going to devastate 'the environment'. On both counts it's acceptable (sustainable would be the more hallowed description) to use modest quantities of flowers in cooking. Florence White, like her predecessors, dries, pickles, preserves, crystallises, vinegarises, fries and ferments flowers in recipes that stretch from a simple lozenge of red roses (a thick-set jelly of pulped petals and sugar 'cut into what form you please') to rococo variations on the Full Salmagundy, an elaborate seventeenth-century conceit consisting of dozens of pickled vegetables, flowers, fruit, chopped eggs and meat, arranged in ornamental layers. Nasturtiums were the favourite flower in this, as they are in salads now.

This is where I must strike a note of caution. Flowers are delicate things. They collapse to a papery mush when wet or at the mere thought of molten sugar. Their fragrances penetrate ingredients you do not want them to, and evaporate altogether in too much heat. I once tried to make a Salmagundy, and I know. The broom buds and nasturtiums stood on their little plates underneath the capers and orange slices and pickled red cabbage. Watercress billowed round mounds of cucumber and pickled herring and cold potato, on plates propped up even higher. If only I had possessed – or known of the existence of – a salad drier. If only I hadn't added so much dressing. By the time it was ready to eat, the Salmagundy looked like a thawing Technicolor snowdrift, as livid vinegars and salty effusions percolated down from the upper layers and turned the crisp heaps of flowers and fruit to slush.

Another debatable recipe quoted by Mrs White is from *The Receipt Book of John Nott. Cook to the Duke of Bolton* (1723). It's for elderflower fritters, but the blossoms were put through such a process of assault and battering that they must have resembled small weathered knobkerries: '. . . lay them carefully in a Soup Dish; break in a stick of cinnamon; pour on them a Wine Glass of Brandy; and when this has stood a minute or two, add half a pint of Sack, stir the Flowers about in this liquor, cover them up, and let them soak about an Hour . . . when the Batter . . . is made, set a quantity of Hog's Lard in a Stewpan; when it is very hot, fry the Fritters.'

A more respectful method would be to use a Japanese-style *tempura* batter. This is a fritter recipe for false acacia, or locust-tree, flowers *(Robinia pseudoacacia)* with their heavenly bean scent. (Wistaria flowers can be used instead, or, of course, elder flowers.)

Acacia flower beignets

FOR 2 PEOPLE

iced water

2 tablespoons plain flour

2 tablespoons rice flour

salt

1 egg

sunflower oil

bunches of flowers from false acacia,

about 10 to 12cm long

Have ready a glass of very cold water, preferably with ice cubes in it. Make a *tempura* batter by mixing together the plain and rice flours with the salt, and stir in the egg. Add the cold water gradually, stirring gently until the batter is moderately runny. For a light *tempura* batter it's important not to beat or whisk vigorously, and there is no need to remove all the lumps. Put the batter in the fridge until you're ready to use it.

Put oil into a deep pan to a depth of about 5cm, and heat up to 165°C on a kitchen thermometer. Sweep the acacia flowers through the batter until they are well coated. Allow any excess to drain off for a few seconds, then slide gently into the hot oil. The batter should start simultaneously to bubble and brown, and the beignets are ready when they are golden-brown, in about 2 minutes. Don't add too many flowers at once, or the temperature of the oil will drop.

Serve with lemon juice and caster sugar.

PS: This recipe also works with fleshy-petalled roses, and with firm green leaves such as comfrey.

Corse libre

CORSICA is legally a French department, but almost every name in the telephone directory is Italian — as the island itself was until the nineteenth century. The inhabitants reject both attachments and insist that they are Corsican. We stayed there one spring, and found that sense of independent identity percolated into the cooking. It had touches of Italian, whiffs of French, but an upstart quality entirely its own. We were based in Calvi, on the west coast, and from our window we could look in one direction and watch dolphins playing in the Mediterranean, and, in the other, see the steep swell of the Haut Asco mountains, still touched with snow on the peaks. The whole town felt condensed, a place where mountain tanginess had been brought down to sea-level.

It was Easter week, and in the early evenings we kept hearing the distant sound of male singing, an eerie, skirling polyphonic chanting. One evening we followed it to its source, up into the old town and along the narrow streets to the Oratoire St Antoine. Inside, the local working-men's choir were rehearsing for the Good Friday midnight procession. We recognised some of the waiters from the local restaurants, having an hour off from their late shift. What they were singing was Corsica's ancient, indigenous choral music – modal, male *a capella* singing, broken by wild solo improvisations that seemed full of Moorish and Celtic echoes. Out in the streets at midnight on Good Friday it had a piercing clarity and authenticity – which was oddly heightened by the fact that our waiters still had their trainers on under their monkish cassocks.

Corsican food is polyphonic as well, based around a few clear, simple but subtle ingredients that are woven together in surprising combinations: wild herbs and spring vegetables; a sheep's curd cheese called *brocciu*; chestnuts (but that's another story – see page 114); fritters and *flans;* pig and wild boar and all the charcuterie that are made from them. Overleaf are a couple of recipes we picked up, the second from a local anthropologist, Félicienne Ricciardi-Bartoli, who is exploring the island's redoubts and collecting local recipes. (There are more Corsican recipes in the chestnut chapter.)

Curd cheese

This is a lemony approximation to *brocciu*, made without rennet.

2 litres full-cream organic ewe's milk
(if you can find it – cow's if not)
5 tablespoons lemon juice
1 teaspoon salt

Damp the bottom of a heavy-bottomed saucepan with water (which helps prevent the milk burning), and add the milk, lemon juice and salt. Warm gently up to 80°C (you'll need a thermometer for this), only stirring if you think the milk is sticking. Small curds should have formed by this time, floating in a yellowish whey.

Strain through muslin (or a pair of tights) and leave to drain overnight. The next day fold the cloth over, and press the whole parcel under a weight for couple of hours, to expel more whey. Don't be disappointed if the amount (about a cupful) of cheese remaining isn't enormous; it's very velvety to compensate, and slightly tangy from the lemon. If well wrapped, it will keep for a week in the fridge.

Nine-herb fritter (Frittelle incu l'erba)
FOR 4 PEOPLE

This is an old Corsican dish, traditionally made with nine different herbs, both wild and cultivated. Feel free to include others, if any of the ones below are unobtainable, but try to keep a balance between bitter, sweet, sour and aromatic.

2 eggs
600g plain flour
20g baking powder
salt
3 large handfuls of 9 mixed herbs: wild mint, sweet camomile
(leaves), dandelion, chard, parsley, basil, garlic, shallot,
penny-royal (just a snatch)
olive oil

Beat the eggs, flour, baking powder and salt together with just a little water, until there are no lumps remaining. Beat in more water, little by little, until the batter is the same thickness as custard.

Chop all the herbs finely and mix well with the batter. Warm a little oil in a non-stick frying pan, and pour the mixture in. Fry for about 10 minutes, turning once, until there is no more uncooked batter visible when you insert a fork.

Spring mushrooms and morel values

SHIRLEY CONRAN'S notorious quip 'Life's too short to stuff a mushroom' provided a fashionable excuse for the whole fast food industry: three millennia of beautiful, brilliant legerdemain with food were microwaved in half a dozen words. One wonders what she considered a more proper use for a short life.

It's painful, therefore, to admit that in one sense she was right, not because of the puritanical saving of time but because the subtle aromas of most mushrooms are best savoured by cooking them simply, alone. But that's not the point. The performance is what's important. Getting stuffing inside such small and convoluted vegetables is as delicate an art as building ships in bottles. Or taxidermy.

But first you must catch your mushroom. These days, beginners are encouraged to join 'forays' in the company of an expert guide, but these are far from a new invention. Even in Britain they've been practised for a century and a half. Among the pioneers was the Woolhope Field Club in Herefordshire, a band of leisure-rich amateurs on the cutting edge of Victorian natural history. Their *Proceedings* for the autumn of 1869 describes an expedition by thirty-five of their members (nine of them vicars). They ranged around the local countryside by carriage, stopping off at likely hunting grounds, measuring the diameters of fairy-rings, and gathering an extraordinary hoard of wild mushrooms: milk-caps, chanterelles, witch's butter, hedgehog fungi. The day ended in the Green Dragon Inn in Hereford, with the exhibits strewn out on the tables, and a late lunch of the day's most enticing trophies: shaggy parasol on toast, fried puffball slices, and fairy-ring champignons in white sauce. The giant puffballs (excellent subjects for stuffing, by the way) were voted a particular success.

This was an autumn outing, in fungi's own season. Spring foraging is a sparer activity, though less so than it used to be, now climate change is compacting late spring, summer and early autumn. In April there is the St George's mushroom, a rich and mealy, almost pure white species of old grassland. Oyster mushrooms (the bracket fungus that is the most frequently sold species in shops, after common mushrooms) will have been on the trees all winter, while another bracket, the sulphurous, lava-like chicken of the woods, will just be beginning to exude from the trunks. By late May the first horse mushrooms will be appearing, and, a few weeks later, the first ceps.

But the most prized of all spring mushrooms, and the hardest to find, is the morel. It's finicky about where it grows, one species – *Morchella vulgaris,* the best-tasting – having an association with ash trees, another, the common morel, *M. esculenta,* preferring chalky or sandy soils. It also has a curious liking for areas which have been burned, and there were many records of morels turning up on bombsites during the last war. I found my first specimens growing from the steps of the parish church in Wenhaston in Suffolk, where there is a fire-and-brimstone medieval painting of the Last Judgement.

But if morels are scarce, they are at least unmistakable, with caps like a spherical or conical mass of honeycomb. They are also delectable, with a rich and aromatic savour, something like a sweet cep. No wonder they've become the grail for US fungus foragers. Mushroom hunting is hugely popular in rural America, but is a much more organised business than in southern and eastern Europe. There are mushroom journals and a plethora of local societies, and most of them seem to regard the morel as 'the Cadillac' among mushrooms. In Minnesota it's been voted the State Fungus, and you can buy comic postcards of outlandish specimens of *Morchella gigantica,* which sometimes weigh in at over 90lb.

But US 'shroomers' don't seem overly interested in the cuisine of the morel, and usually just add to them to existing dishes, such as soups and quiches. There's not even much agreement about how they taste. 'Mushroomy', for sure, but also 'nutty', 'meaty', 'woodsy', like 'thinly sliced sirloin steak' or 'steamed fresh clams'. The more reflective pickers stress not the intrinsic taste, but the savour of 'gatheredness' that hangs about them like an aura. It's a heady cocktail, a blend of atmospheric flashback, the smell of the day, the rush of discovery, the mellowing self-satisfaction of a job done. These were the feelings of one excited morel gatherer in an article in the journal *Mushroom* entitled, 'Morel, May Apples and the Meaning of Life': 'Suddenly it is there in the shadows. A single, exquisite morel, almost six inches high, stands by itself boldly etched against the edge of the orchard. Awestruck, at first, I am afraid to move it. Perhaps it is the last morel in the world. Perhaps it will fall apart to my touch. Perhaps it is only an illusion after all.'

If you are spared such transcendental encounters in the woods, you can buy dried morels online from many gourmet outlets, though they are expensive. They lack the honey fragrance of the fresh caps, but have just as rich a savour when reconstituted and used in cooked dishes. But used fresh or dried, all morels need cleaning first. Their labyrinthine caps are a magnet for sand and mould and the occasional small insect. You should stir them about in cold water for a few minutes, and take them out very carefully, so that any debris is left behind in the water. The bigger ones should be cut in half, the smaller ones used whole.

They can be fried, served with cream, put in meat stews. Antonin Carême, in his *Art de la cuisine française aux dix-neuvième siècle* (1833–5), makes the audacious suggestion of serving them in a ragout with fried herring roes. And Alice B. Toklas describes how she and Gertrude Stein were served a mushroom and cream flan in the countryside near Chartres one spring, when the mushrooms must have been morels: 'While waiting for lunch to be cooked, we walked in the forest where Gertrude Stein, who had a good nose for mushrooms, found quantities of them. The cook would be able to tell us if they were edible. Once more a woman was presiding in the kitchen. She smiled when she saw what Gertrude Stein brought for her inspection and pointed to a large basket of them on the kitchen table, but said she would use those Gertrude Stein had found when she was preparing our lunch.'

But morels are paramountly the mushroom for stuffing. Their heads – unusually for a mushroom – are entirely hollow, and slit in half lengthways reveal a gap like the inside of an egg-shell.

Stuffed morels

as many large morels as you can find or buy,
(this recipe won't work with small specimens)

For the stuffing:
equal quantities of fine white breadcrumbs and
grated Parmesan cheese
garlic
olive oil or melted butter
lemon juice
parsley
seasoning

I've given no quantities in this recipe, as you can't be sure how many
fresh specimens you may be able to find (or afford). Remove the
stalks from the morels so that there is a round hole at the bottom of
the caps. Clean them by soaking (see page 65). Dry, and make a rough
guess about the amount of stuffing needed to fill their interiors.

Make the stuffing with equal quantities of breadcrumbs and
Parmesan, and then make a little binding liquid with dashes of olive
oil (or melted butter) mixed with lemon juice, salt, pepper, chopped
parsley and chopped garlic. Use the minimum quantity of this liquid
– maybe as little as a tablespoon – to just bind the stuffing. The taste
of the morels is too good and unusual to overpower with other

flavours. Fill the morel shells through the stalk hole, using a small spoon.

Place the morels in a well-greased oven dish. Place generous knobs of butter on top of each one and replace the lid of the dish, or, if it doesn't have one, seal with foil. Bake in an oven at 180°C/gas 4 for 30 minutes.

Morel and butter bean stew
FOR 2 PEOPLE

This is a recipe from Sam and Sam Clark, of Moro restaurant, who adapted it from a Turkish original. The combination of fungus and butter beans sounds improbable, but it works, chiefly because of the wonderful collision between these two warm and oddly-matched ingredients, and a cold sharp salad.

100g dried butter beans
150g fresh morels, or 40g dried
olive oil
lemon juice
1 clove of garlic
½ a red onion
a mixture of chopped sweet herbs – basil, tarragon, parsley, dill, whatever you can find, amounting to about 2 tablespoons in all

12 ripe cherry tomatoes
salt and pepper

Dried butter beans are so incomparably better than tinned that going through the longer preparation needed is worth it. Soak the beans overnight in a large bowl of water (they expand quite a lot).

Next day drain the butter beans and set them to simmer for about 40 minutes in clean water. Meanwhile rinse the fresh morels, or soak the dried ones in water for an hour, to clean and reconstitute.

Make the dressing by beating together in a bowl 2 tablespoons of olive oil, a tablespoon of lemon juice and 1 crushed clove of garlic. Chop the onion with the herbs, slice the cherry tomatoes into quarters, and mix both with the seasoned dressing.

When everything is ready, keep the beans warm in their cooking liquid and fry the morels in olive oil for about 5 minutes, until they are soft. (The dried ones may take a little longer.) Add the beans, and bring briefly to the boil. Then remove from the heat and fold in (don't stir too much) the dressed tomatoes. Serve immediately.

Summer

Bright colours, luxuriant produce, high temperatures. The signature fruit across the globe is the tomato; in Britain, the pod-pea and the runner bean. If you're lucky, there's a glut of vegetables, which is a kind of waste if not fully used. Spicy weather is as well matched by spicy food as by cool salads (as all tropical cuisines understand). Eastern ways of cutting and recooking are a godsend in fecund heatwaves, creating new ways with proliferating ingredients.

*

Heading East

I FIRST ATE Chinese food when I was a student in Oxford in the 1960s. I know what I had, because I had exactly the same dish the next week, and the week after, and not simply because it was the cheapest thing on the menu. Chicken chop-suey with crispy noodles – varied occasionally by chicken chow-mein with *soft* noodles – had me by the throat, as if it were some kind of addictive noodleburger. I had no idea at the time that the dish had probably been cooked up in America to satisfy Western tastes. It certainly satisfied mine, by having two quite new texture sensations in one dish: the pallid crunchiness of beansprouts, like eating the very essence of vegetable before it had taken particular form; and the contrasting crispness of the roasted or deep-fried (I didn't know which) noodles. A snappy pasta. I was intrigued, too, by this staple existing in two different forms. Allotropes, we would have called them in school chemistry.

Years later, when I began to explore Chinatown in London, and gaze at the dried ducks hanging in the restaurant windows, the notion that Chinese chefs were above all conjurors with heat began to settle in me. Not that I had dared try any Chinese heat magic myself. I was not even very clear about how you ate the food, let alone cooked it. The first time I ordered crispy duck in a Gerrard Street restaurant, I set about it as if it were a kind of bistro duck salad: mouthful of duck, bit of cucumber, dip a pancake in the plum sauce. The manager watched me with increasing exasperation, and in the end – echoing that pushy Spanish waiter a decade earlier – strode across, nudged my chair sideways, and made a proper roll for me: plum sauce on centre of pancake, bits of duck on top (nicely balanced flesh and skin), add strips of cucumber and spring onion, fold and roll. It was all there, in every single bite.

Later still, I discovered Japanese cuisine, and used to sit at the bar table, watching the chefs slicing sashimi and making extraordinary sculptures in fruit with just a few deft nips and tucks. I was amazed at how raw ingredients, manipulated in this way, could be made so *accessible* to the tastebuds, even though I'd learned as a child that the way you sliced vegetables influenced their taste. But I could see now that it was not so much pure taste which was affected, as what you might call 'the experience in the mouth'. A carrot sliced thin and on the diagonal, for instance, exposes a large area not just to the tongue but to the roof of the mouth. Once cooked it has the elastic 'give' of a wafer. You're as likely to suck it as chew it. The aromatic softness drawn through the mouth is part of the 'taste'. At the other extreme, thick chunks, cut on the round, involve the teeth from the outset, and the textural sense is of rougher, abraded surfaces. Flavour comes from the inside of the vegetable as well as its exposed outer parts. In both cases, flavour, smell, texture and 'mouth-touch' (and expectations conjured up by the appearance of the food) are so intermingled that the act of eating is almost synaesthetic.

At this point, alas, my inner scientist – the earnest sixth-former with a nerdish interest in reducing phenomena to simplistic patterns – re-emerged. I thought that if Chinese cooking was about the metamorphoses wrought by heat, Japanese was about surfaces, and the transformations induced by pressure. Chemistry and physics, respectively.

It was a ludicrous generalisation, not least because Chinese cuisine is every bit as dependent on artful cutting as Japanese. But as a guide to learning some cooking techniques useful for any ingredients in any kitchen, I'll stand by it as a rule of thumb, with sincere apologies to those two great cuisines.

Below are two dinners. The Chinese involves using the techniques of air-drying, double-cooking, and stir-frying. The Japanese involves fine cutting, pressure, and a lot of regard for colour.

Peking Duck
FOR 4 PEOPLE

I first made this on a very cold winter's day in Norfolk, with the duck hanging up between me and the blast of Polly's mum's old fan-heater. It's better as a summer dish, but less energy efficient if the fan isn't warming a freezing room as well as cooking the duck.

1 free-range duck, about 1.5kg

For the glaze:
1 lemon
500ml water
2 tablespoons honey or brown sugar
3 tablespoons soy sauce
130ml dry sherry or saki

Slice the lemon, rind included, and bring to the boil with the rest of the glaze ingredients. Simmer for about 20 minutes. Using a ladle or large spoon, pour this mixture over the duck several times, until the skin is completely coated. Hang the duck over a tray (I strung mine up from the back of a chair), into which the remainder of the glaze liquid has been poured, and direct a fan on it, at lowest heat, for about 4 to 5 hours. If you don't have a fan-heater, hang the duck close to a radiator in a well-ventilated spot. In the early stages, ladle more glaze over the bird if there are patches which look dry or uncovered.

The skin will gradually start to brown and stiffen, until it is the consistency of parchment. Transfer the duck (breast side up) to a roasting pan, with just a little water in it, and place in an oven pre-heated to 240°C/gas 9. After 15 minutes, reduce the heat to 180°C/gas 4 and roast for another hour.

Carve — skin included — into bite-sized pieces, and serve with *hoisin* sauce, sliced spring onions and cucumber, and some Chinese pancakes. You can make these with a batter of hot water and flour, but personally I would cheat and buy them.

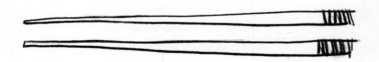

Twice-cooked belly of pork
FOR 2 PEOPLE

Double cooking is an ancient Chinese process for rendering out some
of the fat from greasier meats, and ideal for summer meat dishes

500g belly of pork, cut into ribs
oil

For initial simmering:
2 thin slices of root ginger
3 spring onions
1 teaspoon five-spice powder
salt

For stir frying:
sunflower oil
3 cloves of garlic
1 red pepper
2 leeks
1 small onion
2 tablespoons chicken stock
2 tablespoons hoisin sauce
1 tablespoon dry sherry or saki
1 tablespoon soy sauce

Put the pork into a casserole dish with the ginger, spring onions, five-spice powder, and salt to taste, and just cover with water. Close the pot with a tight-fitting lid (use foil between the lid and the pot if necessary), and simmer for about an hour, either on top of the stove, or in an oven at 130°C/gas ½. Remove, drain through a colander and discard the liquid, spring onions and ginger.

Heat a tablespoon of oil in a frying pan with a lid, or a shallow casserole dish, and stir-fry the belly pieces for about 10 minutes, until they are browned. Spoon out any extra fat rendered up. Then add the garlic, red pepper, leek and onion, all thinly sliced, and continue frying for 2 or 3 minutes. Add the chicken stock, hoisin sauce, dry sherry or saki, soy sauce and salt. Place the lid on the pan and braise on a low heat for a further 10 minutes.

Serve with plain boiled rice, and stir-fried summer salad (overleaf).

Stir-fried summer salad
FOR 4 PEOPLE

This is a stir-fry using European salad vegetables, and goes well with any summer meat dish as well as with Chinese food.

2 slices ham or bacon
2 cloves of garlic
1 handful of mint leaves
mixture of summer salads, including different colours and spicy leaves, e.g. Pallo Rosso, dandelion, Little Gem lettuce, rocket, Mizuna, lamb's lettuce, etc., about 2 large handfuls altogether
1 tablespoon sunflower oil
salt
black pepper
sherry vinegar
soy sauce

There is one essential stir-frying principle. The oil in the wok or pan must be very hot when it makes contact with the ingredients to be fried. This is why they must be kept constantly in motion, by shaking the pan and stirring with a wooden spoon or spatula, so that new material is constantly brought into contact with hot oil. If you have a lot of vegetables to stir-fry, either do them in small batches, or keep scraping open an area at the base of pan, to which you can introduce new bits.

First make all the ingredients ready. Chop the bacon into pieces about 1 cm square. Squash and roughly chop the garlic, and tear the mint leaves into small pieces. Wash and tear the salad leaves into large pieces.

Heat the oil in a wok until it is just begining to smoke. Add the bacon cubes and fry for 2 minutes. Add the garlic and mint leaves and stir-fry for a further minute. Then throw in the salad leaves and stir very vigorously until they are just on the point of wilting. Finally sprinkle with salt and pepper, add a dash each of sherry vinegar and soy sauce (they should hiss and steam immediately), toss a few more times and serve.

*

The following three Japanese dishes are all served cold and are all vegetarian. They make a fresh summer supper.

Spinach rolls
FOR 2 PEOPLE

This is spinach metamorphosed. The compression of the leaves changes their usual flaky texture into something quite fleshy. But choosing the best time to make the rolls poses a bit of a dilemma.

They taste best with young, new season spinach in early summer, but are easiest to make once the leaves are over 30cm long. Compromises are always possible.

Pick or buy 2 large bunches of spinach. Wash well and remove any brown patches, but leave the stalks on. Tie the bundles up, wrapping a string spirally around them. Boil a large saucepan of water and plunge the two bundles into it, blanching for no more than 3 minutes. Remove (using the ends of string, if you're dextrous enough) and cool rapidly under the cold tap, which helps maintain the bright green colour.

When the leaves are fairly cool begin to squeeze the water gently out of them, forming the bundles into long club-shapes. When all the water appears to have gone, remove the string. Lay each bundle on the edge of a tea-cloth and roll it up, squeezing as you go. Continue rolling, as if you were working a rolling pin. When you eventually open the cloth, you should have a neat green cylinder.

Cut into segments about 4cm long, and serve cold, with soy sauce.

Quick pickles

Japanese cuisine is full of pickles, many made over weeks in tubs of rice bran. But it also includes same-day pickles, bright and unusual additions to summer meals, hot or cold. The technique works with any firm vegetable. Peppers, mushrooms, cauliflower, radish, spring onions, cucumber, cabbage, French beans. Lemons and plums, and root ginger, too. Pickle them separately, or mixed. The products are remarkably crisp and vinegary, despite the speed with which they're made.

> vegetables and/or fruit of choice, about 500g
> 1 cup of rice wine vinegar
> 2 tablespoons sugar
> salt

Slice the vegetables into strips no more than 5mm thick and 1cm wide, cutting on the diagonal to expose as much surface as possible to the pickling liquid. With cucumbers, remove the skin, and scrape out the mushy seed layer. With French beans, try cutting them along the seam with a thin-bladed knife, so that you have two matching halves. With plums, simply cut in half and remove the stone.

Bring a saucepan of water to the boil and plunge the vegetables (and fruit, if used) in. Leave for no more than 5 seconds, then drain them and rinse them under a cold tap. Dry, spread out on a plate, and sprinkle them with salt, to begin drawing out the water. Turn them around with a spatula from time to time to make sure the salt covers all surfaces.

Meanwhile, put the vinegar, sugar and 2 teaspoons of salt into a small saucepan and bring to the boil. Take off the heat and allow to cool slightly. Pour over the vegetables, and toss them lightly in it. Put another plate – preferably identical to the first, so that there's a good fit between them – on top of the vegetables, face up. Put a brick or other weight on top, and leave for 4 to 6 hours.

Drain the pickles through a sieve before serving, and rinse them slightly if you don't like too much salt in your food. Serve with rice or fish, or with the salad below.

A summer salad
FOR 2 PEOPLE

This was inspired by a Japanese 'autumn salad', in which the muted colours of the ingredients were intended to suggest the mellowness of the season. This is an adaptation for summer, using primary colours. It relies partly on the pickling effect above.

3 or 4 long radishes, preferably white

1 sweet red pepper

½ a cucumber

4 or 5 spring onions

sugar

rice wine vinegar, or white wine vinegar

3 eggs

salt

sunflower oil

a small bunch of watercress

Cut the radishes and the pepper into quarters, then slice into strips about 5cm wide and 5cm long. (A kitchen hatchet is almost essential for this.) Do the same for the cucumber, scraping away the seeds and inner pulp, but retaining the skin. Mix all these vegetable sticks together on a plate and sprinkle with salt, to draw out some of their moisture. Leave for about 30 minutes, turning once or twice with your hands.

Drain the vegetables and pat dry in a cloth. Transfer them to a bowl, sprinkle with sugar, and add enough vinegar to cover them.

Now prepare the egg. The intention is to produce a much drier, more granulated scramble than conventional breakfast eggs. Beat the eggs with a little sugar and salt. Heat a splash of sunflower oil in a non-stick pan, add the eggs and stir continuously over a low heat. The object is to finish with eggs which are the consistency of fried rice or couscous, and this may take up to 5 minutes. Mash well with a fork, transfer to a bowl, add 2 tablespoons of vinegar and mix well. Drain the vegetables and stir into the egg.

Shred a bunch of watercress by hand on to a plate, and strew the vegetable-egg mixture on top.

Glut

'Never give away zucchini to your true friends in July'
(Californian proverb).

'There are more ways to cut a courgette than the Japanese
have knives' (Norfolk ditto).

THE INGENUITY of making-do is as important for dealing with
excess as it is for coping with scarcity. Gluts of vegetables and
fruit are one of the mixed blessings of good summers. When conditions are just right – early rain for peas, a late heatwave for tomatoes,
say – there can be bumper commercial harvests which bring prices
right down in the shops (or at least in small greengrocers and farm
shops). We ought to buy seasonal vegetables in quantity when they're
cheap, and refuse to be bound by conventional recipes. Preserve them
by pickling, drying and freezing, but rethink them as immediate food
sources as well. Try tomatoes simmered until they are sweet enough
for a dessert. Use chard leaves for wrapping savouries, as if they were
vine leaves.

But gluts in your own garden, arriving with the unstoppable
momentum of junk mail, can be an embarrassment, compounded by
the fact that the same phenomenon is being experienced by your
neighbours, too. Down country lanes in July little stands begin to

appear in front of houses, as normally diffident cottagers are converted into street traders by the effusions of runner beans and marrows and gooseberries.

In the larger scheme of things, of course, there is no such thing as glut. It all goes to a nobler cause than one's own greed. Pigeons strim the unruly spinach, shrivelled peas drop off and join the great commonwealth of the soil, the shredded broccoli leaves turn the wretched caterpillar into the exquisite butterfly. Even those irrepressible and eventually maddening courgettes can find a new meaning for themselves. One summer our vegetable garden was ringed with self-sown plants, each one bearing single round fruits in the joints between leaf and running stem, at intervals of roughly a metre. It was a plant unlike any we had ever sown, but with an uncanny resemblance to the wild American gourd (*Cucurbita pepo*) from which the entire dynasty of marrows and pumpkins has been bred.

But such high-minded and selfless detachment doesn't come easy in a fecund garden in July. Every neglected and abused sprouting quivers with moral reproof. You started me off, it says, what are you going to do about me? The idea of 'waste', at this moment of confrontation, is objectionable. Waste is profligacy. Waste puts up food bills. Waste is all that time spent planting and weeding, when you could have been lounging in a hammock.

But the right response isn't self-evident. You're tugged one way by a sentimental (or frugal) reluctance to pluck your babies before their prime, and in the other by an aesthetic desire to do the vegetable justice, to have it at its best moment. Courgettes are the most troubling vegetables in this comedy of dilemmas, because their prodigious rate of growth demands you make trade-offs between size and succulence. I suspect most growers respond in the same way. The first two or three fruits of the summer, the courgettes *nouveaux*, are treated like votive offerings, picked when they're no more than eight

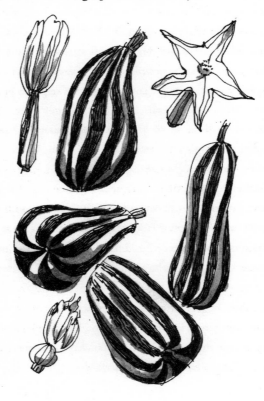

centimetres long, steamed whole for a couple of minutes, and then not so much chewed as sucked, like exquisite green blancmanges. You leave the rest to 'put on a bit of body' and in a matter of days you're overrun. You pick what you need but, frugally, choose the biggest, which are already too big. Within a week the bed is full of beached vegetable whales, and for the next two months you play catch-up, convincing yourself that the big ones are now really marrows, and can be left even longer. There can be a frisson of relief when, some time in late summer, they just stop producing. Except that, lurking in the leaf-shadows, their blistered peel like green sharkskin, are more monsters that have been swelling unnoticed for weeks.

One answer to gluts – and courgette gluts especially – is surgery. Reinvent the recurring vegetables with the knife. Expose their soft centres. Use them as receptacles. Regard them as a kind of pasta – or meat. Carve and mince them. Cut them in any way that will make them behave differently in the pot, and then in your mouth. This isn't meant to be purely cosmetic surgery, though I suppose that you could, *in extremis*, become a vegetable whittler. (The Chinese do this with the swedes sometimes used to ornament crispy duck platters.)

Here are a few recipes based on slicing, hacking or otherwise dis-membering courgettes in different styles, arranged in order from total pulverisation to simple bisection. They all use about half a dozen courgettes, or 1kg, depending on size.

Courgette soup

FOR 2 PEOPLE

For the floppiest, most tired and overgrown fruits. This is from our friend Pooh Curtis, whose village responsibilities in Blakeney regularly involve her in cooking for hundreds.

2 medium onions
4 cloves of garlic
butter
1kg courgettes
1 litre chicken or ham stock (see page 174)
25g butter
curry powder
salt and pepper
250g fromage frais, or soft cheese

Slice the onions and garlic finely, and gently fry in 2 or 3 spoonfuls of butter until they are golden. Add the sliced courgettes (peeled first, if the skins are old and tough). Then add the stock. Bring to the boil, and simmer until the courgettes are quite soft. Add a dessertspoon of curry powder, salt and pepper to taste, and the *fromage frais*. Liquidise until smooth, and serve either ice cold or slightly warm, not hot.

Courgettes rapées
FOR 2 PEOPLE

Best with small and firm courgettes.

1kg courgettes
salt
2 tablespoons olive oil
parsley

Cut off the tips of the courgettes but don't peel them. Grate them coarsely (with a *hand* grater: a food processor is liable to turn them into a moist mush), spread them out on a clean tea-towel, and sprinkle them with salt. Leave for about 45 minutes, turning the gratings a few times, then fold the ends of the towel and press down to squeeze out as much water as possible. Twist the towel ends together and finish by wringing the gratings dry. Heat the oil in a shallow pan, add the courgette gratings and a tablespoon of chopped parsley, and fry for about 10 minutes, turning with a wooden spoon. The courgettes are ready when they're golden; brown is overdone.

Zucchini tagliatelle al l'arrabbiata
FOR 2 PEOPLE

Courgettes have a kind of substantive relation with pasta. They're pale-fleshed and absorbent. Larger pieces become flexible when cooked. Cut in different shapes they can be substituted for everything from penne to lasagne. This recipe needs quite long courgettes, a minimum of 18cm.

ripe tomatoes, about 1kg
1 whole red chilli
50g smoked ham
4 cloves of garlic
extra virgin olive oil
1kg courgettes

Make the arrabbiata sauce first. Skin the tomatoes by pouring boiling water on them, leaving them for a few minutes, then peeling them under a cold tap. Slice in half, cut out the larger white cores, and scrape out the seeds if you wish. Put to one side. Chop a whole red chilli very finely, crush the garlic, and slice the ham into 1cm strips. Fry these gently together in 2 or 3 tablespoons of olive oil for 5 minutes, until the garlic begins to colour. Add the tomatoes, and simmer for 15 to 20 minutes, stirring and squashing the mixture

until it forms a slightly lumpy purée (push it through a sieve if you prefer it smooth).

Top and tail the courgettes and remove the skin with a potato peeler. You now need to slice off long strips of the white flesh about 1mm thick, the courgette tagliatelle. The modern safety-razor type of peeler will chamfer slices which are too thin, but an old-fashioned blade model will work. Alternatively use a sharp thin-bladed knife, standing the courgette on end and sliding the blade downwards, so that you end up with an octagonally shaped core. Stop peeling when the pith and pips become visible.

Get a wide saucepan of water on a good boil and throw in the courgette strips. Bring back to the boil and simmer for no more than 90 seconds. Drain, and add the reheated arrabbiata sauce.

Char-grilled courgettes
FOR 2 PEOPLE

Suitable for larger specimens, 20cm x 8cm.

1kg courgettes
olive oil

Top and tail the courgettes, but don't peel. Cut them lengthwise into slices 1cm thick. Brush the slices on both sides with olive oil. Heat a griddle, or a large non-stick frying pan, until it's very hot, add the courgettes and sear for a few minutes, turning from time to time. Depending on size, they will be ready in between 4 and 8 minutes. Serve hot or cold. They make a sumptuous cold starter or salad ingredient, having taken on an almost meaty texture. Dress if you like with a sprinkle of sherry vinegar, or with crushed garlic, parsley and salt.

PS: Try serving these – together with char-grilled slices of aubergine – with lemon juice and a sprinkle of sugar as a dessert. They are oddly reminiscent of pancakes.

Stuffed courgettes
FOR 2 PEOPLE

Suitable for overgrown courgettes and small marrows.

1kg courgettes
1 medium onion
6 spring onions or a small bunch of chives
about 250g feta cheese
juice of 1 lemon
salt, black pepper and chilli powder or cumin to taste
olive oil

Strip off the hardest outer layer of the courgette with a peeler, but leave the ends on. Cut in half lengthways, and scrape out the pips and pulp with a spoon – again leaving the ends intact (this is to ensure a tight seal when the two halves are put back together).

To make the stuffing, chop the onions finely and mix with about the same volume of crumbled feta. Do this with a fork rather than in a blender, to retain some texture. Work in the juice of a lemon, and add salt, ground pepper, and a touch of chilli powder or cumin, if you like. Spoon this mixture into the hollowed courgette halves, filling them level with the cut surface – but don't worry if there isn't enough stuffing. A few gaps won't matter. Put the two halves back together, making sure they are the right way round, and truss up with string, like a joint of meat. Brush with olive oil, put into a baking tin, and cook in an oven preheated to 170°C/gas 3 for 40 minutes. The stuffed courgette emerges with the majestic presence of a baked carp, slightly glazed and caramelised on the surface.

Alternatively, omit the oil, wrap the trussed courgette in foil, and cook for the same time. This gives a silkier, more aromatic result. Serve by cutting in vertical slices about 5cm thick.

If you're lucky enough to get hold of some round courgettes, there's no need to wrap them at all. Simply slice the lids off, hollow out with a spoon, and insert the feta and onion stuffing. Return the lid, and pin on with toothpicks. Then bake as above.

Picnics

S MALLER COURGETTES, stuffed like the ones opposite, are good picnic morsels. If the courgettes are more than about 5cm wide, hollow them out with an apple-corer rather than splitting them in two, and push the stuffing in through the end.

The challenge of all good portable food is to make the containers edible themselves, without sacrificing their efficiency as holders – which is why the sandwich will always be the basic picnic standby. Peppers are inefficient as carriers, because their mouths are too wide. Aubergines are too fragile, once they've been cooked.

Salad sushi

Salads are always a problem on picnics, because of the physical way-wardness of the ingredients. The lettuce leaves go limp, the tomatoes burst, there's nowhere to put the dressing.

One way of making them genuinely portable (with a respectful nod to Hill's 'salad-ball', page 44) is to tie up bunches of leaves with seaweed.

fresh-picked sea-lettuce, oarweed or kelp; alternatively, dried
Japanese seaweed (wakame, kombu and nori are all good – the
important thing is that the seaweed is in long wide strips)

mixture of salad leaves, red and green

chives, parsley, stalks included

sea salt

pepper

Wash fresh-picked seaweed well, slice into strips about 3cm wide,
and boil for 10 minutes. If using dried seaweeds, reconstitute and
cook according to the directions on the packet.

Lay a handful of the salad leaves in parallel, with a few stems of
chives and parsley. Sprinkle with a little salt and pepper (but no oil)
and turn into a tight bundle by rolling the sheaf under your hands on
a board.

Wind one or two strips of seaweed round each bundle of salad.
They should be flexible enough to tie up with a knot. Wrap the base
of each bundle with damp tissue, if you want to keep them really
fresh.

Eat with your fingers, dipping into a little sea salt on a plate.

Spinach lasagne with Mediterranean vegetables

FOR 4 PEOPLE

This is a way of using another potential glut vegetable – spinach – in place of pasta. It makes an exciting and light lasagne, good for anyone who has problems with wheat or gluten. Polly's recipe includes chorizo sausage, but this could also be left out if you want a dish proof against just about every food sensitivity.

courgettes, aubergines, red peppers and red onions,
in any proportion
olive oil
sea salt
a few cloves of garlic
1 to 2 red chillies
½ a tin of chopped tomatoes
coriander and basil leaves
nutmeg
about 10 large spinach (or chard) leaves
100g chorizo sausage
a handful of grated Cheddar
250ml crème fraîche
1 egg

Slice the courgettes and aubergines diagonally into 1cm thick pieces. Quarter the peppers and remove the cores. Slice the onions lengthways, again to provide 1cm thick pieces. Lay the vegetables in a roasting dish, sprinkle with olive oil and sea salt, and bake in an oven at 180°C/gas 4 for about 30 minutes.

Meanwhile, fry a few sliced cloves of garlic and 1 or 2 red chillies in a litle olive oil until the garlic is just beginning to colour. Stir in the tomatoes, some torn coriander and basil leaves, and a little grated nutmeg, and simmer for about 10 minutes. Put the sauce to one side.

Remove most of the stalk from the big spinach leaves, without tearing them in two if possible. Fold them gently over so that they will fit in the top of a steamer, and steam for 2 minutes.

Take a dish about 8cm deep, wipe the base with oil, and put a layer of the roast vegetables at the bottom. Smear with a spoonful of the sauce, then lay a couple of sheets of spinach on top. Now make a layer of thinly sliced chorizo, smear with sauce, and add two more spinach sheets. Continue the alternation until all the ingredients are used up.

Make a topping by whisking together the cheese, crème fraîche and beaten egg. Pour on top of the dish, and bake in an oven at about 140°C/gas 1 for 30 minutes.

Green gazpacho
FOR 4 PEOPLE

This is a salad soup, a summer stock-pot for green leftovers.

any mixture of lettuce, chicory, cucumber, green pepper,
mint, chives
4 cloves of garlic
4 tablespoons olive oil
salt and pepper
2 thick slices of dry white bread, soaked in water

Chop the lettuce and chicory roughly. Peel the cucumber, cut it in half lengthways and scrape out the seeds with a spoon. Quarter the green pepper and remove the seeds and ribs. Place all the salads and herbs in a food processor with the garlic, olive oil, salt and pepper and bread. Whirl until they form a smooth green paste.

Transfer the contents to a liquidiser, and begin to add water slowly, blending all the while, until you have a soup with the consistency of single cream. Pour into a serving bowl and cool in the fridge for at least an hour. Serve with croutons.

Beanfeast

A GLUT OF RUNNER BEANS is one of the easiest to bear. Served alone with butter as a starter, steamed with a roast joint, sautéed Catalan-style with garlic, oil and new potatoes, runners don't tire easily. The problem comes when the green shells become harder and the strings stringier. There's no easy way of reviving the flesh, as there is with old courgettes. It is simply too hoary to eat. But the seed beans inside are still soft and edible, and one summer we

started taking these out of their pods and experimenting with ways of using them on their own. It was hardly an original move – many European beans are used as both pod and seed – but doesn't appear to have been tried with the scarlet runner.

The runner bean's fortune in Britain had been turned around by improvisation before. It was introduced here from America in Charles I's time, by the great plant hunter John Tradescant. The trusses of scarlet flowers were looked on as purely ornamental at first: 'Ladies did not . . . disdain to put the flowers in their nosegays and garlands.' It was the ingenious Philip Miller, keeper of the Chelsea Physic Garden, who first had the idea of eating the young pods, some time in the mid-eighteenth century.

Polly and I thought we might carry this story a stage further, and treat the late scarlet runner as a source of carbohydrate. Even shelling the pods proved a treat. The beans popped out satisfyingly with runs of the thumb, and looked like birds' eggs in the bowl. They were all subtly different, depending on their age and variety. There were pale cream ones, some mottled in mauve or pink, many with black freckles on a purple ground. To begin with, we started using them straight from the pod, with boiled bacon and onions. The liquid they made was so lustrous and succulent, we drank it straight as soup the next day.

But there was more to come. The beans we didn't use immediately dried easily by being laid out on trays in the boiler room for a couple of weeks. And when we came to clear the beans from the beds in early autumn, we found so many shrivelled, unpicked pods that we were able to fill another huge bowl with vine-dried beans.

Now this is a regular autumn harvest. They see us through the winter, and while they are still comparatively young they have as much texture and taste as many imported beans, such as cannellini, that are grown specifically for drying.

The Full English Cassoulet
FOR 4 PEOPLE

The cooking of beans with various kinds of meat is popular in vernacular cuisines across the northern hemisphere. The Spanish classic *fabada asturiana* mixes giant *judia* beans with salt pork, bacon and sausage. Kentucky Burgoo is a long-cooked stew of lamb, chicken, lima beans and corn. The Dutch *bruine bonen* is a winter stew of brown beans, bacon and vegetables. In southern France there is the best-known beanfeast of all, the *cassoulet*. Britain, alas, seems to have had no such national bean and pork dish – though we enjoy tinned baked beans with bacon and sausage, especially at breakfast.

This is a *cassoulet* adapted for British ingredients. It is best with freshly podded beans, when it produces a dish light enough for a late summer supper.

500g fresh beans (from scarlet runners) or 250g dried beans

2 medium onions

olive oil

bay leaf

garlic

500g smoked and preserved meats, made up from a selection of
the following: smoked bacon or gammon, confit of duck,
pork boiling sausage (Cumberland sausage is ideal)

500g fresh meat, made up from a selection of the following:
chicken drumsticks, pork ribs, neck of lamb fillets

1 small can of chopped tomatoes

white wine

salt and pepper

breadcrumbs (optional)

If you are using dried beans, soak them overnight in cold water. If
they are more than one year old, boil them for an extra hour, saving
the liquid.

Slice the onions thinly, and simmer in a saucepan with a gout of
olive oil till they are golden. Add the beans, bay leaf and several cloves
of squashed and rough-chopped garlic. Cover with water (using the
pre-boil liquid if you have reconstituted the beans), bring to the boil
and simmer for half an hour. Add the boiling sausage, chopped into
bite-sized pieces, and simmer for a further 30 minutes. Drain, saving
the liquid, and put aside the sausage and beans on a plate.

Dry the pan, add a little more oil, and brown the remaining pieces of meat (bacon, chicken, lamb, duck etc.). Add the tomatoes, a splash of white wine, salt and pepper, and bring to the boil.

Put half the bean and sausage mixture at the bottom of a casserole dish. Make the meats and their accompanying sauce into a second layer. Strew the remaining beans and sausage on top, and add enough of the saved liquid to just cover them. Sprinkle with breadcrumbs if you fancy a crusty top.

Put on the lid and place in an oven preheated to 150°C/gas 2 for 2 hours. Check once or twice, and if necessary top up with a little more liquid or wine. Remove the lid, sprinkle the top with olive oil, and bake at 180°C/gas 4 for a further 20 minutes.

Serve with a green salad and plenty of red wine. And a fried egg on top, if you want the utterly Full English.

Going with the grain

B READ IS THE human species' most remarkable food invention. It is also the ultimate processed food, the result – even 4,000 years ago – of no less than four transformations of its raw material: milling, dough-making, leavening and baking. Children adore it almost as soon as they're weaned (the crust has that half-burnt savour – the Fifth Taste – that our species finds irresistible), and societies across the globe have turned it into the world's most widespead staple food. It's cheap, filling, nutritious, and durable.

Bread and arable agriculture co-evolved. The fact that grain crops (such as the *Triticum* grass species from which wheat was developed) produce their seed heads at a more or less even height above ground meant that they were amenable to harvesting *en masse*, and eventually to mechanisation. The rootedness of the crop, growing in a fixed spot for more than half the year, led to the development of settled communities, and then to the evolution of the town, which in turn increased the demand for a convenient staple like bread. Arable-based societies had more free time – and free hands – than hunter-gatherers, and used them to develop skills as diverse as literature and war. It wouldn't be an exaggeration to say that Western civilisation, as we understand it today, couldn't have evolved without bread and the agriculture which underpinned it.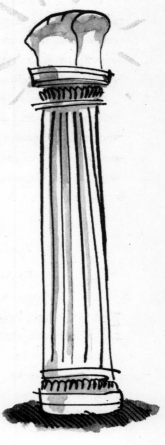

Here then are a few recipes to celebrate the Staff of Life.

Mesopotamian bread

Make this as an adventure in historical re-enactment. It's no delicacy, but was probably the first deliberately risen bread in the world. I've cobbled together the recipe from the clues given in a group of cuneiform tablets recently unearthed from Yale University's Babylonian Collection.

A bread culture was well established in Mesopotamia by the second millennium BCE. Unleavened bread was made in a clay hearth, by sticking flattened doughballs on to the hot walls (much as pizzas and nan bread are traditionally made) or, more elaborately, by mixing the dough with milk, oil and herbs, and baking in ceramic dishes.

Leavened bread was being made long before the isolation of yeast. The rising agent was sometimes a meat broth that had been allowed to go sour, but more often rough beer, which always contains some wild yeast. Predictably, for a culture in which grain crops were central, brewing was developed before wine-making.

This version is made from spelt flour (spelt and emmer are two of the earliest cultivated wheat types) and real ale. Don't make the mistake, as I did on my first experiment, of using pasteurised light ale, which is virtually yeast-free.

500g spelt flour
1 teaspoon salt
400ml unpasteurised ale (a barley wine, or 'White Label' type
with plenty of sediment, is the best)

Mix the flour and salt in a bowl. Warm the beer (slowly, otherwise the froth will overflow) to about 50°C, and add gradually to the flour, mixing it in and then kneading it firmly. Use a food processor and a dough-hook if you fancy (I often do), but take the dough out and enjoy the last few kneads by hand.

Allow to rise *for no more than 10 minutes*. The wild yeast seems to be fragile, and becomes progressively less active. Knead again briefly and shape into a rough flattish loaf. Place it on a flat metal tin. Put it into a preheated oven at 220°C/gas 7 and blast at this heat for 5 minutes. Then turn down to 200°C/gas 6 for a further 30 to 35 minutes.

Don't expect a loaf as light and aerated as one made with refined pure yeast. But this heavy Mesopotamian bread is crusty and flavoursome (if understandably beery), and you can understand why the primordial bakers persevered.

Rye soda bread

Recipes for breads made with other kinds of flour usually recommend that you mix in wheat flour, to give more elasticity to the dough and a better rise with yeast (which reacts with the gluten in wheat flour). This really isn't necessary with rye flour, which does contain some gluten, and which can be risen perfectly adequately with baking powder. This rye bread can be made from start to finish in an hour and a quarter, and is dense, dark, fragrant, and best eaten freshly baked.

500g rye flour
2 teaspoons bicarbonate of soda
2 teaspoons cream of tartar
1 teaspoon salt
1 tablespoon olive oil
250ml milk (or water)

Mix together the flour, soda, cream of tartar, salt and olive oil. Add the milk or water gradually, kneading until the dough is pliable. You may need a little more liquid, depending on the quality of the flour. (If you are using a dough-hook with a food processor, the dough is ready when most of it sticks to the hook as a single ball.) Leave to stand for 30 minutes. Then bake in an oven preheated to 200°C/gas 6 for 35 minutes.

Moroccan flatbread

A very easy bread, lighter than pitta, and good with most Middle Eastern and North African dishes.

500g strong white bread flour
1 teaspoon salt
15g yeast
325ml warm water
2 tablespoons olive oil

Mix the flour and salt in a large bowl (or use a food-processor's dough-making facility). Dissolve the yeast thoroughly in the warm water, and gradually add to the dough, working it in by hand or dough-hook as preferred. Then add the olive oil, and work that in.

Transfer to a floured surface, and knead well for a further 3 or 4 minutes. The dough should be springy and elastic, so work in a little more water if not, or more flour if it is sticky. Set aside, covered with a cloth, to rise for 1 hour.

Preheat an oven to 220°C/gas 7. Divide the risen dough into four pieces, dust a rolling pin and board with flour, and roll out each quarter until it is about 3 to 5mm thick and the shape of an oblong. Transfer to an oiled tray (or two if necessary) and bake for about 8 minutes. The flatbread should be brown and slightly crisp on the outside, but soft and pliable inside.

*

But there was a darker side to the triumph of bread. The worldwide spread of an agricultural technique developed for the deserts of the Middle East has been the modern Earth's greatest single ecological disaster. The creation of arable fields demands, first, the complete obliteration of the forest, with all its wild species and ecosystems. The vanished trees (burnt, as often as not) contribute to atmospheric carbon dioxide, and are no longer there to absorb it. The tilling of the soil, which opens up unoxidised organic matter to the air, also liberates huge quantities of carbon. The first evidence from ice cores of unnatural amounts of CO_2 entering the atmosphere dates from about 10,000 years ago, just the moment when the first farmers began their long – and still running – project of forest clearance, burning and ploughing.

These homogenising processes, the simplifying of a three-dimensional landscape to a two-dimensional, and of a complex biological system to a monoculture, became worse with mechanisation. Deep ploughing caused soil erosion and sometimes created dustbowls. Pesticides and artificial fertilisers put paid to the few remaining wild species that clung on in arable fields. Monocultures encouraged disease and infestation, and thus even more potent chemical responses. The *reductio ad absurdum* of the arable ideal is a cultivation system which takes the crop out of the rigours of the natural world altogether, and hides it under sheets of polythene dozens of acres in extent, transforming the crop from an outgrowth of the fields to a kind of back-growth, or premonition, of the shrink-wrapped packaging of the supermarket shelf.

But there has always been an alternative. Time for the forests to answer back.

Autumn

Fruit scents, crisp nuts, another whole harvest.
Apples, almonds, aromatic quince. But not always mellowness.
There's sharpness, too. Frost-bloomed damsons and aniseed-scented
mushrooms. Autumn can bring a second glut, too, so fruits and
nuts can become staples, vehicles for reducing our dependence
on intensive arable farming. The making of jams and preserve
is still a national pastime, so I've not touched much on it here
(see page 218 for books on this and on autumn toadstools).

*

Fruiting forests

THE HUMID MOUNTAIN forests that stretch between western
China and the Middle East are the home of large numbers of
the temperate zone's edible fruits and nuts. Apples, walnuts,
apricot, pears, quinces, mulberry, plums all had their wild origins
here. No wonder they are often called 'fruit forests', and that there
are lively cultures entirely supported by their produce – and by the
honey that is a by-product of the tree blossoms, and the browsing
animals that feed on windfalls.

This three-dimensional farming — 'forest farming' as it's usually known — is attracting interest worldwide because of the way it's able to provide staple food without destroying landscapes and ecosystems in the way that arable agriculture does. In Europe it has long been practised, especially in chestnut forests. Chestnuts are the most viable European alternative to cereal crops, containing 70 per cent carbohydrate and often cropping at up to 3 metric tonnes per acre without chemical assistance and on very poor soils — a figure far in excess of wheat in comparable conditions.

Chestnuts

THE SWEET CHESTNUT probably evolved on the western edges of the fruit forests, maybe in eastern Turkey. Its names — chestnut, *castanea* in Latin, *châtaigne* in French — derive from the name of the ancient city of Kastanaia in Anatolia. The tree is now widespread in Europe.

We first came across chestnut culture in the Massif des Maures in Provence. The granite Massif's dense forests are full of wild chestnuts (and extraordinary butterflies, bee-eaters, boar and harvested cork-oaks) but also managed chestnut orchards. In these, wild trees have been used as stocks for ancient grafts of productive chestnut varieties. They show signs of regular pruning too, like filigree pollards.

In the museum at Collobrières we bought a packet of chestnut flour, but the assistant assured us it wasn't much used in local cooking any more. This was, I think, a piece of wool-pulling, a defence of a local delicacy, maybe, or a reluctance to admit that such a peasant staple was still in use in affluent Provence. In the years that followed we've found chestnuts still in wide use throughout southern Europe – in Corsica, northern Spain, Turkey. In Italy the chestnut forests have been at the centre of whole cultures, with the flour supplementing wheat in bread, the timber used in house building, the small wood for fuel, and the blossoms generating one of the richest honeys in Europe. In the Lot, our friend Jean has told us how chestnuts were so economically important when he was a boy that the schools gave pupils time off to harvest them. He longed to be in the library instead. But this studious man hasn't deserted the local

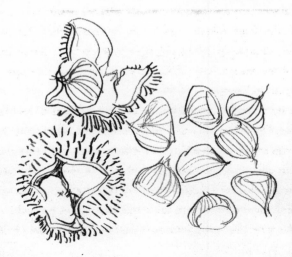

manna. At his village's annual chestnut festival he mans a rotary roaster converted from the insides of a washing machine. In all these places we found chestnut's warm, woody, aromatic savour permeating stews and soups, cakes and breads.

The French recognise two basic kinds of chestnut: *châtaignes*, which are the wild nuts, and *marrons,* the larger fruits of the grafted and tended orchard trees. These are bigger, and tend to fruit with just one or two nuts per husk. Chestnuts were probably brought to Britain by the Romans, have never been improved, and rarely grow to the size of those raised in warmer climates. But they are still useful, and can be used in any of the dishes requiring whole nuts below. They are one of the crops that ought to be seriously considered for a Britain faced with a warming climate and competing demands on land for food and conservation.

A note on sources and preparation

Sweet chestnuts are traditionally gathered from the ground in October and November, and the shiny nuts removed from the spiny husks by stamping on them with stout shoes. To prepare the nuts, prick the skins and roast them in hot embers. (But leave one unpricked. When that bursts with a crack, the others are ready.) Alternatively boil them for half an hour in their skins. Either way of pre-cooking makes it easier to remove the skins, and the slightly bitter fibrous sheath below.

If you can't gather your own chestnuts, vacuum-packed, pre-cooked nuts are excellent.

Chestnut flour you have to buy ready-milled. Shamefully, it isn't easy to obtain in Britain, even though it is the carbohydrate of choice for all people with gluten sensitivity. Badger your health-food store, chemist, delicatessen, to get a regular supply.

. Chestnut in all its forms is so versatile, it can form the backbone of an entire cuisine Here are a few examples.

Pulenda
FOR 4 PEOPLE

This is cooked Corsican chestnut-meal, close enough in function to Italian maize-meal, *polenta,* to have an equivalent name. It's used as a kind of rough bread, and is served with *brocciu* (see page 59) and meat casseroles.

1 litre water

salt

500g chestnut flour

Bring the salted water to the boil in a heavy saucepan, then put in all the chestnut flour in one go. Simmer gently and stir continuously with a narrow wooden spoon, or porridge stick (there is a bespoke wooden spatula called a *pulindaghju*), until it forms a smooth, lump-less paste. Keep stirring energetically (it's hard work), and the *pulenda* will form a ball round the spoon or stirrer and begin to bubble on the surface. (This whole cooking process may take 20 to 30 minutes.) At this point remove the dough from the pan with a knife or spatula. Allow to cool, then knead it for a minute or two. Roll it out on a board dusted with chestnut flour, and into the form – as the local dictum has it – of *un grand saucisson*. Then cut it into slices about 2cm thick with a narrow knife – or, if you want to be truly Corsican, with a length of string.

Pulenda can be served cold, reheated or fried.

Chestnut bread

300g strong white bread flour
150g chestnut flour
salt
1 packet of yeast
olive oil
390ml water

Mix the wheat and chestnut flours with a heaped teaspoon of salt, either in a large bowl, or in a food processor's dough-making bowl.

Dissolve the yeast in a mixture of 260ml just-boiled water with 130ml cold, stir in 2 tablespoons of olive oil, then slowly add this liquid to the flour, mixing and kneading as you go. Remove from the bowl, and knead for a further 4 minutes on a floured board. Cover with a cloth, and leave to rise in warm place for 2 or 3 hours.

Heat the oven to 220°C/gas 7. Cut the dough into two pieces, knead again for a minute or two, shape into rough loaves, and put into buttered loaf tins. As soon as they are in the oven, reduce the heat to 200°C/gas 6. Bake for 30 minutes, until the base of the loaf sounds hollow when tapped.

PS: This recipe works just as well with nuts such as hazel, walnut and almond, minced for 2 minutes in a food processor. Best of all are pecans, whose natural oils give the loaf's crust a delectably crisp nuttiness.

Chestnut and porcini soup
FOR 4 PEOPLE

250g chestnuts (tinned will do)

30g dried porcini (better than fresh for this soup)

1 large onion

4 rashers of bacon

100g butter

lemon juice

fino sherry

Peel the chestnuts, if you are using fresh ones (see page 116), and boil for an hour in a large saucepan with just enough water to cover (40 minutes will do if you're using vacuum-packed nuts). Reconstitute the dried porcini in sufficient boiling water to cover them, and leave to soak for 30 minutes. Hang on to the water.

Meanwhile peel and finely slice the onion, cut the bacon rashers into broad slices, and fry both in the butter for about 10 minutes, until the onion is golden. Then slip this mixture, plus the porcini and their soaking water, into the pan containing the chestnuts and their water. Simmer for a further 15 minutes.

Cool the soup a little, and liquidise in batches until it's thoroughly smooth, adding water if necessary until it is at your preferred consistency. Reheat in the pan with a squeeze of lemon juice, and just before serving add a small glass of fino sherry.

Chestnut stew
FOR 2 PEOPLE

Use any ordinary stew recipe, replacing some of the meat with fresh or vacuum-packed nuts, and the dusting flour with chestnut flour. Here is one recipe.

500g venison, pheasant or beef
a small handful of chestnut flour
olive oil
2 medium onions
4 rashers of bacon or strong ham
4 cloves of garlic
2 bay leaves
strips of orange peel
1 large glass of red wine
salt and pepper
250g chestnuts

Cut the meat into 3cm cubes, and dust in chestnut flour. Heat a splash of olive oil in a casserole and brown the meat, turning frequently for about 5 minutes. Remove to a plate. Slice the onions and bacon and fry in the same pan until the onions are golden, adding more oil if necessary.

Return the meat to the dish and add the garlic, bay leaves, orange peel, red wine, salt and pepper. Top up with water (or more wine, if you fancy) so that the meat is just covered. Put into an oven preheated to 150°C/gas 2, and cook for 2 hours. Add the chestnuts after the first hour. Check the level of the liquid once or twice, and top up if you like a runny stew. Or don't if you prefer a thick gravy.

Serve with boiled potatoes and carrots roasted in the oven along with the casserole.

Chestnut pancakes
FOR 4 PEOPLE

We were e-mailed this recipe by a man who'd sold us chestnut flour in the market of Grignan in Provence.

125g chestnut flour

2 eggs

pinch of salt

250ml milk

butter

Beat the flour, eggs and salt in a bowl with a little of the milk, until you have a smooth, thick batter. Beat in the remainder of the milk. Allow to rest for an hour. Melt a little butter in a non-stick pan and heat until it just begins to smoke. Pour a ladleful of batter into the pan, and immediately swirl it round to cover the pan's whole surface. Fry until the underside is freckled (about a minute). Toss, or turn with a spatula, and fry the other side. Serve with lemon juice.

Chestnut has an affinity with orange, and you can make a variant of crêpe Suzette with the pancakes. Put a mixture of butter, 2 table-spoons of orange juice, a teaspoon of finely grated orange peel and a small glass of Grand Marnier or Curaçao into a large pan, and simmer for 2 minutes. Fold the chestnut pancakes in four and place them in the mixture. Keep on the heat, and pour over them another glass of Grand Marnier, Curaçao or brandy. When the alcohol is bubbling well, light with a match and stand clear. Shake the pan gently so that all the alcohol is burnt off. Serve immediately.

Chestnut flan (Pasticciu castagninu)
FOR 4 PEOPLE

This is another Corsican recipe. The first time I made it I assumed it was served hot, and was mortified that it emerged from the oven with the consistency of sloppy blancmange. Fortunately the next day it had set like an egg custard, which it essentially is – a French *flon,* so to speak, rather than an English flan.

100g chestnut flour

750ml milk

150g sugar

butter

4 eggs

Put the chestnut flour, milk and sugar into a saucepan and heat gently, stirring frequently until the flour lumps have vanished. Continue to simmer, just short of boiling, until the mixture becomes quite thick (about 10 minutes).

Line a round oven dish, about 5cm deep, with greaseproof paper, and rub a little butter over the paper. Beat the eggs in a bowl, and stir into the chestnut mixture. Pour into the dish and bake in an oven at 160°C/gas 3 for 40 minutes. Leave to cool overnight, or for at least a few hours, and turn upside down on to a large plate before serving.

PS: Chestnut flour can be substituted for wheat flour in almost any recipe, provided you add baking powder to help it rise a little. Try it, for instance, in a Yorkshire pudding, cooked under the meat.

More nuts

White gazpacho, ajo blanco
FOR 4 PEOPLE

ALMONDS were one of the staples of our schooldays' hunter-gatherer economy. The trees had been planted as ornamentals along our road, and fruited well, though the kernels were never very big. We were oblivious of the fact they were an extraordinarily balanced food (21 per cent protein, 55 per cent fat, 14 per cent carbohydrate) and just relished bashing the bitter-sweet kernels free of the shells.

Almonds are another denizen of the fruit forests, and have been spread across the temperate world. This is a nectarous summer soup from Andalucia, of Moorish origins probably. The classic *ajo blanco* recipe suggests grapes simply as a garnish. But I find that using them to provide most of the liquid for the soup is a revelation.

225g blanched almonds
2 slices of white bread, decrusted and soaked in water
4 cloves of garlic
3 tablespoons olive oil
a small bunch of seedless white grapes
salt and pepper
sherry vinegar

Grind the almonds in a food processor until they begin to stick to the side of the bowl. Loosen them a little with a spatula, and add about 5 tablespoons of water. Turn the processor back on, and whirl until the almonds form a paste which begins to fold back on itself. Squeeze as much water as you can from the bread, and add the bread to the almond paste along with the garlic. Whirl again until smooth.

Transfer the contents to a liquidiser, blend in the olive oil, and then add the grapes a few at a time, blending all the while. Add seasoning and extra water if necessary, until you have a soup with the consistency of single cream. Pour into a serving bowl and cool in the fridge for at least an hour.

Serve with a garnish of halved grapes, and splashes of sherry vinegar.

Bisteeya – or a little something to do with almonds and leftover chicken
FOR 4 PEOPLE

When I first read about this great Moroccan festive dish, a fantastic concoction of almonds, meat and eggs wrapped in pastry that's found nowhere else in the world, it sounded quite uncookable, demanding arcane skills and ingredients quite beyond me. In fact it's easily manageable, provided you're patient and work slowly. And if the cooking is an adventure, so is the eating. Cutting into the complex, multiple layers of this dish is like exploring a new ecosystem.

500g cooked chicken (or 1 small whole chicken)
1 medium onion
½ flat teaspoon each of ground ginger, cinnamon, saffron,
allspice, salt and pepper
4 eggs
chicken stock
200g almonds (blanched or peeled)
225g butter
9 sheets filo pastry
icing sugar to decorate

If it's not cooked already, boil the chicken for 1½ hours with the onion and all the spices. Save the stock. If you have pre-cooked or leftover chicken, make the stock separately with a stock cube and 500ml of water, plus the spices and the chopped onion. Whatever its origins, cut the cooked chicken into bite-sized pieces.

Beat the eggs with 100ml of the chicken stock, and season with salt and pepper. Pour into a small frying pan and stir slowly over a low heat until the mixture is creamy and just beginning to set. Remove from the heat.

Blend the almonds until they are almost a paste, and simmer them in butter for about 10 minutes.

These three ingredients – chicken, eggs and almonds – constitute the filling of the pie. Choose a pie or oven dish about 25cm wide and 5cm deep. Melt about 200g of butter in a small saucepan and keep it warm and molten. Brush the inside of the dish with the butter, and place a sheet of filo pastry in it, so that it overlaps the rim. Lay 3 more sheets on top (in different directions, so that all the dish is lined), brushing a little melted butter on to each layer. Then spread the almonds over the top layer. Spread half the egg mixture over the almonds and sprinkle with 2 or 3 tablespoons of the stock. Cover with 2 more sheets of filo, each one lightly brushed with melted butter. Lay the pieces of chicken on the filo. Moisten the chicken well with more stock, and then spread the remainder of the eggs on top. Cover with 3 more filo sheets, brushing each one with butter. Then tuck up the whole dish, folding the top filo sheets inside the pie dish. Bring the overlaps of the bottom and middle sheets up alternately and fold over the top. Brush with melted butter between each fold, and on the last top sheet.

Bake in a preheated oven at 180°C/gas 4 for 40 minutes. Then raise the temperature to 200°C/gas 6 for a further 15 minutes, by which time the pastry should be crisp and golden.

Decorate with sprinkled icing sugar and cinnamon, and serve hot.

A good acompaniment is quick-preserved oranges (see page 80 for general technique). Slice 2 oranges into thin segments, ½ to 1cm thick. Plunge them into boiling water for 2 minutes, then drain and spread them on a flat plate. Sprinkle well with salt, and turn from time to time. Meanwhile, bring a cupful of white wine vinegar, 2 tablespoons of sugar and 1 tablespoon of salt to the boil. Allow to cool a little and pour over the salted oranges. Stir them together well, and make into a flat layer on the plate. Put another plate — preferably identical — on top, with a weight on top of that. A brick is ideal. Leave for at least 6 hours, then strain. Check a piece for saltiness, and rinse the remainder quickly if necessary.

Salade Aveyron

A highly local salad, which seems not to have spread to either books or restaurants outside its birthplace in south-west France. It features two of the specialities of the region, Roquefort cheese (a blue ewe's cheese) and walnuts — another wonder food, with 18 per cent protein, 61 per cent fat, 14 per cent carbohydrate.

2 Little Gem lettuces (or other good-hearted variety)
250g shelled walnuts
250g Roquefort cheese
walnut oil
lemon juice
salt and pepper
sugar
garlic

Cut the lettuces into quarters lengthways and place in a salad bowl. Crush the walnut kernels with your hand, so that there's a mixture of large and small pieces. Add to the lettuce. Then crumble the Roquefort over them. Whisk 2 or 3 tablespoons of walnut oil with the juice of 1 lemon, salt, pepper, a pinch of sugar and a couple of crushed garlic cloves. Pour over the salad and mix well.

First fruit

THE APPLE is probably the best-known fruit, though it is not the mythological first fruit. (Eve's apple must have been a quince or fig to have fruited in the heat of Mesopotamia.) It is certainly one of the most widespread and most versatile of fruits. There may have been as many as 20,000 different varieties of apple developed around the world, in a range of flavours and degrees of sweetness and sharpness that has made them adaptable to everything from rich soups to tart pickles.

Yet the apple seems oddly, patriotically English, as natively rustic as rosy cheeks. Richard Bradley wrote in 1718: 'There is no kinds of Fruit better known in England than the Apple, or more generally cultivated. It is of that Use that I hold it almost impossible for the English to live without it, whether it be employed for that excellent Drink we called cider, or for the many Dainties which are made of it in the kitchen.' In *Food for Free* I followed conventional wisdom and took it for granted that the domestic apple had in some mysterious way evolved, or been bred from, the sour little native crab apple. There was, after all, a wealth of circumstantial evidence, stretching from neolithic archaeology to Shakespeare's crab-apple songs. But it was a lazy assumption, based on romanticism and no evidence whatsoever. It's now clear from DNA analysis that all domestic apples originated from a single species, *Malus pumila*, native to the fruit forests of central Asia (see page 131), and that no other species were ever hybridised with it in its long journey to become the most widespread fruit in the world.

The pome's progress was finally disentangled by the distinguished botanist Barrie Juniper. It looks as if an aboriginal apple species in the forest of Tian Shan in western China, round-fruited and long-stalked, was subject to strong evolutionary pressures, partly by the constantly changing topography of the mountain ranges, and partly because of interaction with browsing animals. Bears were quite likely the chief agents – the midwives if you like – in the birth of the domestic apple. They would have repeatedly selected the sweetest and largest wild apples, scattering and manuring their pips, and gradually boosting these qualities in the local gene pool. But apples never grow entirely true from their pips, and the huge variability of this emerging new species, *Malus pumila*, lived on in the fruit forests.

These mutable fruits (again, selected for sweetness and size) were taken west by migrating tribes, and the wild trees followed in their wake, springing in all their unpredictable diversity from cores and pips, often in the dung of early horses, which, like bears, adore apples. Then, about 4,000 years ago, someone in Babylon discovered grafting. It was another of those apocryphal Eureka! moments, inspired, in the legend, by the glimpse of a natural graft between two chafing branches. Whatever prompted the invention, it was now possible to perpetuate these fugitive varieties by surgically implanting their branches on to another apple tree.

Every one of the tens of thousands of apple varieties that subsequently spread across the world is just a happenstance sport of that single Asian species, spotted by a shrewd fruitarian, and perpetuated by grafting.

Three thousand years on, the great English gardener John Parkinson drew up a euphonious list of some of the offspring of this long tradition, including:

The Gruntlin is somewhat a long apple, smaller at the
   crowne than at the stalke, and is a reasonable good apple.
The gray Costard is a good great apple, somewhat whitish
   on the outside, and abideth the winter.
The Belle boon of two sorts winter and summer, both of
   them good apples, and fair fruit to look on, being yellow
   and of a meane bignesse.
The Dousan or apple John is a delicate fine fruit, well
   relished when it beginneth to be fit to be eaten, and
   endureth good longer than any other apple.
The Pot apple is a plaine Country apple.
The Cats head apple tooke the name of the likenesse, and is
   a reasonable good apple and great.

My old friend the gardening writer Francesca Greenoak, whose book *Forgotten Fruit* (1983) pioneered the revival of old fruit varieties in Britain, remarks that as well as its revelations of the lost shapes and colours and times of fruiting, this list is a kind of poem: 'There is a reasassuring substantiality in the measured cadences of the seventeenth-century sentences.'

Henry David Thoreau was an avid forager, and added another poetic layer to the diversity of the fruit nation. In his posthumous book *Wild Fruits* (published in 2001, but written in 1859–60) he hoists a flag for that intangible quality of 'gatheredness': 'The bittersweet of a white-oak acorn which you nibble in a bleak November walk over the tawny earth is more to me than a slice of imported pine-apple.' When recalling 'Going a' Graping' it's the ones he couldn't reach that filled him with the wildest delight. 'What is a whole binful that have been plucked to that solitary cluster left dangling inaccessible from some birch far away over the stream in the September air, with all its bloom and freshness.'

Recounting his quest for American apple species – and American wildings (feral trees sprung from discarded or bird-sown pips or cores) – he draws up a litany of varieties defined not by botany, but by where they grow, the moment they are picked, the mood of their pickers:

> . . . the apple which grows in dells in the woods (Malus sylvestrivallis) also in hollows in pastures (Malus campestrivallis); the apple that grows in an old cellar hole (Malus cellaris) . . . the Truant's Apple (Malus cessatoris), which no boy will ever go by without knocking off some, however late it may be;

the Saunterer's Apple – you must lose yourself before you can
find the way to that; the Beauty-of-the-air (Malus decus-aeris)
. . . the Green Apple (Malus viridis), this has many synonyms:
in an imperfect state it is the Cholera morbifera aut dysten-
terifera, puerulis dilectissima . . . the Railroad Apple, which
perhaps came from a core thrown out of the cars; the apple
whose fruit we tasted in our youth; our Particular Apple, not to
be found in any catalogue, Malus pedestrium-solatium; also the
apple where hangs the forgotten scythe.

Thoreau also recommends picking the sourer wilding apples – from
the tree or off the ground – in December, after they've been frozen
once or twice and then thawed out. The acidity has gone, and the flesh
has turned to a sweet ciderous purée.

But that 'reassuring substantiality' was not proof against
aggressive modern commerce. Both the genetic diversity of apples
and their evocative dwelling-places have been trashed for the past
half-century. The presumptions made by supermarkets about our
tastes and preferences mean that the odd-coloured fruit, the apple
which is naturally blemished, the tree which bears fruit at an incon-
venient time, the original, the idiosyncratic, the local have all been
banished into a kind of apple ghetto, to be kept alive by enthusiasts.
The supermarkets have made cosmetic improvements by enlarging
their range to include a few international alternative brands such
as Gala and Braeburn, but still resolutely refuse to source and sell

locally, compounding their assault on biodiversity by excreting huge amounts of greenhouse gases in transporting their produce.

Yet the old varieties are being rediscovered in ancient gardens and orchards, and are being propagated. The fruit is being sold through farmers' markets and vegetable and fruit box schemes; and more growers need to get their own back for the way the super-markets have exploited them by growing and selling fruit direct to the public.

And one of the greatest reservoirs of genetic variety is the wilding apples that spring from bird-sown fruit or thrown-away cores in hedges and commons and waste ground. Most pips don't grow into the same kind of apple that originally bore them (though a few do – which, as we saw above, is how the apple evolved) but express the huge range of variety intrinsic to the aboriginal *Malus pumila*.

When I lived in the Chilterns I had an Elysian Way of wilding apples, a stretch of ancient green-lane that wound south into the hills. I discovered it from the smell of one of the apples, which reached fifty metres: a lemon-yellow fruit, with a scent like quince, too acid and hard to eat raw, but spectacular with roast meat. Another had the bitter-sweet effervescence of sherbet; a third bore long-pear-shaped apples, whose sharpness overlaid a warm smoky flavour, as if they had already been baked. Somewhere, somone may redis-cover the sixteenth-century John-Apple, which was reputed to keep for two years; or the fabulous fennel-scented Reinette de St-Ogne.

If you are using bought varieties, do your bit for biodiversity by choosing local specialities. Books like *The Apple Source Book* (2007) will help, as will local Apple Day markets. My Chiltern speciality was Lane's Prince Albert, which originated in my own home town of Berkhamsted in the mid-nineteenth century, and was named after the Prince Consort, who was visiting the town at the time. In south Norfolk it's Captain Palmer, a small flat apple with fragrant, almost honeydew-melon, pale yellow flesh, raised at Diss in the late nineteenth century.

Pot-roast pork with wilding apples
FOR 4 PEOPLE

The acidity of wilding apples makes them a good foil to the rich fattiness of pork. Instead of a side serving of apple sauce, try cooking them with the meat itself.

2 medium onions
sunflower oil
6 wilding apples (or local variety of cooking apples,
like Norfolk Beefing – Bramleys will do)
root ginger
2 cardamom pods
organic pork, preferably Gloucester Old Spot or
Tamworth (leg or loin, say 1.5kg)
sea salt and pepper
about 200ml cider
1 glass of Calvados (optional)

In a deep casserole dish sauté the finely chopped onions in oil (sunflower for lightness) for about 10 minutes, until they are golden. Peel and core the apples, slice roughly, and sauté with the onions for a further 5 minutes. Add 1 tablespoon of root ginger, thinly sliced or pared with a peeler, and 2 crushed cardamom pods. Put the joint of pork into the casserole, season with ground sea salt and pepper, and add enough cider to provide no more than 2cm of liquid at the bottom of the pot. Seal the top of the casserole with foil before putting on the lid. Cook in an oven at 150°C/gas 2 for about 2 hours.

Open the dish at the table, as the meat will be appetisingly fragrant as well as tender, and add a dash of Calvados before serving.

Apple mash

potatoes
cooking apples
butter
seasoning

Use potatoes and apples in proportion of two to one by weight. Peel and halve the potatoes and bring to the boil. After about 10 minutes add the peeled, cored and chopped apples. They'll both be cooked in another 10 minutes. Drain, return to the saucepan, add a few slivers of butter and some salt and pepper, and pound with a masher or fork. Do not add any extra milk, cream or oil, as there is plenty of liquid produced by the apples.

Jugged celery and windfalls
FOR 2 PEOPLE

This is a wonderful old country recipe, gathered by Dorothy Hartley. It can be used as either a starter or a vegetable with pork or lamb.

equal weight of windfall apples and celery, say 250g each
2 cloves
muscovado sugar
4 rashers of bacon or ham

Wash and trim the apples, but leave their skins on. Chop roughly and stew them with a couple of cloves and a spoonful of muscovado sugar in as little water as possible, until they are a firm pulp. Put a couple of slices of bacon in the bottom of the tallest, narrowest cooking pot you possess, pile the apple purée on top, then pack in as many sticks of celery as you can. They must be in an *upright* position, as it is the apple juices running down the fibres of the celery that makes this dish. (This is why you need a tall casserole, or an old-fashioned stew-jug.) Spoon out any apple purée that overflows, trim the sticks level and cover their tops with 2 more bacon rashers, cut to fit. Then bake in an oven at about 180°C/gas 4 for half an hour.

If you don't have a suitable tall cooking-jug, simply follow this recipe using chopped apple and celery in an ordinary casserole dish.

Apple parchment

Francesca Greenoak dries a lot of her apples for the winter, using a custom-made fan-driven dehydrator with perforated trays. One particulary succulent product is her apple parchment.

Peel, core and slice the apples, and make them into a thick pulp by heating with just splash of water for about 10 minutes (and puréeing in a blender if necessary). Spread this out in the dryer in a thin layer on a flexible plastic mat which fits on to the trays (often provided with dryers). Dry gently for several hours, until the purée has turned to a leathery vellum, which can be peeled off the tray. This can be stored, rolled or flat, and cut up as sweetmeats.

Lamb's Wool

Lamb's Wool is a mixture of hot ale, baked apple pulp, sugar and spice. I came across it in Eric Linklater's brilliant comic novel *Poet's Pub* (number 3 of the original orange-backed Penguins, and first published in 1929), which describes the exploits of the rowing blue and minor poet Saturday Keith as he takes over an ancient inn called the Downy Pelican. One of Saturday's projects was the mounting of an Elizabethan feast for his grotesque guests, which included, 'Kickshawses, Stewed Pike, Roast Sucking-pig, Olive Pie, Roast Capons, Marrowbone Pie'. An accompanying drink was Lamb's Wool. It has some affinity with what was called the Wassail Bowl, which is warm beer put through a second fermentation with brown sugar and yeast, and served with hot roasted apples floating on it. Also with the kind of drink Puck is talking about in *A Midsummer Night's Dream*:

> Sometimes lurk I in the gossip's bowl
> In very likeness of a roasted crab
> And when she drinks, against her lips I bob,
> And down her withered dewlap pours the ale.

FOR 2 SERVINGS

2 large cooking apples
2 tablespoons brown sugar
2 pints of real ale
1 flat teaspoon mixed cinnamon
allspice and ground cloves, altogether

Core – but don't peel – the apples, pour the sugar inside the cored hollow, and bake in an oven at 180°C/gas 4 for about 40 minutes. Remove, and scoop the pulp and molten sugar out of the skins and into a saucepan. Add the ale and spices, and gently warm while whisking the apple pulp in. The drink should have a fine frothy head and be hot, but some way away from boiling.

'Saturday and Joan returned with a bowl that perfumed the room and made all mouths water with its rich October smell . . . Saturday had discovered that even the best apples and the oldest ale are improved by an egg or two beaten up in thin cream with enough whisky to counteract the fatness of the cream.'

Uncooked apple and pear chutney

This is a recipe developed by my brother David from an Australian version, which in turn seems to have originated in the East End of London, to judge from its rhyming-slang nickname 'Stairs Pickle'. It's unusual in being uncooked.

450g sharp apples

450g firm pears

25g root ginger

2 cloves of garlic

450g raisins

450g white sugar

600ml cider vinegar

2 teaspoons salt

1 teaspoon chilli powder

Peel and core the apples and pears, and finely chop with the root ginger and garlic. Mix them thoroughly with all the other ingredients, cover and leave in a cool, dark place for 3 days. Bottle the chutney in sterilised jars. It will be ready to use in about a month.

PS: There is an early Chinese recipe for making apple flour. It's an elaborate process, involving fermentation, sun-drying and grinding.

But given the desirability of tree-grown staples, it ought to be revived. There are fuller details in Barry Juniper's *The Story of the Apple*.

Plums

UNLIKE APPLES, plums have been through a good deal of hybridisation during their evolution. The ancestral species, the wild plum, *Prunus domestica*, originated from an early, natural hybridisation between the European sloe, or blackthorn, *Prunus spinosa*, and the cherry plum, *P. cerasifera*. The place of origin was probably the fruit forests of Iran or the southern Caucasus, where the extreme eastern range of the blackthorn overlaps with the western edges of cherry plum territory. Since then the plum has been taken across the globe and developed into thousands of varieties, including the large groups of damsons and gages. It also occurs in subspecies, like the smaller blue-black or yellow-fruited bullace. All members of the plum family are mutually fertile, and natural hybrids have occurred between plum and bullace, and plum and sloe, with a continuous range of back-crosses between all three. The Victoria was a natural hybrid discovered in a garden in Sussex in the 1830s. The popular commercial plum the Pershore was found in Tiddesley Woods in Worcestershire in 1827.

This doesn't, alas, mean that unpredictable and hugely variable

plum varieties are constantly springing up in woods and hedges. It is rather uncommon to find plum seedlings in the wild, though strays do occur close to orchards and farms. Hybrids are more likely where different kinds of plum grow close to one another, or where they have been deliberately encouraged by artifical cross-pollination. These hybrids may escape into neighbouring copses or waste ground, or be planted out in hedges. They reproduce by suckers more successfully than by seed, and can begin to 'fill up' a hedge. It's these cultivated relics and throwbacks that you're most likely to find in the wild, especially with damsons, which, even in a short stretch of old hedgerow, can crop up in all manner of shapes, sizes and flavours. The Norfolk writer Charles Bryant's *Flora Diaetetica or, History of Esculent Plants* (1783) lists dozens of plum varieties, whose names are as evocative as the apples': White Primordian, White Mogul, Little Black Damask, Apricot Plum, Fotheringham, Red Diaper, Violet Perdigron, Myrobalan, Date Plum, Cloth of Gold.

The types of plum you are most likely to find in the wild are:

DAMSONS The plum from Damascus, hence also Damasks. Usually
dark purple, with a frost-at-midnight bloom, but occasionally
greenish. They occur in all shapes and sizes. We once found a
hedge with damsons as big and round as pullet's eggs. They were
also very ripe, so that picking them was like milking: you simply
put your hand under the clusters and they tumbled in. A few had
fallen on to the stubble in the adjoining field, and become
impaled on the straw like enormous fruit lollies. The bigger
damsons are often sweet enough to eat off the bush, but some
smaller varieties are as sour as sloes, and need cooking.

CHERRY-PLUMS OR MYROBALANS One of the ancestors of all
  cultivated plums. The trees are frequent in woods and hedges,
  and in flower from February (when they're often mistaken for
  early blackthorns). They are scarce fruiters in this country, but
  becoming more regular as the climate warms. The fruits are more
  or less spherical, reddish-orange or yellow, and mild to the taste
  even when raw.

BULLACE A sub-species of *Prunus domestica*. Quite scarce in Britain,
  it has spherical fruits midway in size between sloe and damson.
  The yellowish variety is sweeter tasting than the normal blue-
  black.

Prunes

Easy to make, even with damsons. (I once found branchfuls of
spontaneously formed damson prunes where a hedge had been cut
while in full fruit, and the damsons had dried out slowly in the
autumn sun.) Dry them either whole, or halved and stoned. Spread
them out on trays in the airing cupboard for 2 or 3 weeks, or use a
commercial dryer – which will do the job in about 8 hours. Store
them in airtight jars to prevent them reabsorbing moisture and
catching mildew.

Plum soup
FOR 2 PEOPLE

This is a Polish soup, but despite my mum's Polish ancestry, it never found its way on to our family table.

500g plums or damsons, stoned
500ml water
500ml white wine
a few parings of lemon rind
cinnamon stick
sugar to taste
a cupful of boiled potatoes
sour cream

Put the plums into a saucepan with the water, wine, lemon rind, cinnamon and a tablespoon of sugar and simmer for about 30 minutes. Remove the lemon rind and cinnamon, and taste for sweetness. Add more sugar if necessary. Liquidise, and add about a cupful of chopped, boiled potatoes. Serve with a swirl of sour cream.

Lamb and cherry plum tagine
FOR 4 PEOPLE

I first made this dish with scavenged cherry plums. It was one of those rare years when *Prunus cerasifera* fruited in abundance, suddenly revealing the identity of many previously anonymous hedgerow shrubs. I'd spotted this patch of brilliant scarlet and orange in the lane from a hundred yards away. Close-to it turned out to be drifts of cherry plums, blown out of invisibility by a storm. A few had been squashed by cars, but I was able to pick up nearly 5 kilos of perfectly ripe fruit.

(It is just as good, if a little sharper, made with damsons, but you will need to add 2 tablespoons of sugar during the cooking.)

2 medium onions
50g butter
1 teaspoon cumin seed
1 tablespoon finely chopped root ginger
a few threads of saffron
3 cloves of garlic
1 teaspoon cinnamon
1kg organic lamb, shanks or small leg
500g cherry plums, or garden plums
water, stock or white wine
sloe or damson gin (optional)

In a casserole or thick saucepan, sauté the onions in the butter with the cumin seed, for about 10 minutes, until the seeds have burst and the onions are golden. Add the ginger, saffron, crushed garlic and cinnamon. Cook together for a couple of minutes. Fry the lamb in the mixture quickly, turning it so that all sides are slightly browned and well coated with the spices. Add half the damsons, and about a cupful of water, stock or white wine. Cook gently in an oven at 150°C/gas 2, for 2 hours, checking the level of the liquid once or twice. Fifteen minutes before the end, add the remainder of the damsons and a small glass of sloe or damson gin – if you enjoy the almond taste given by plum-family stones. The liquid should be appreciably thicker at the end (give it a sharp boil for 5 minutes on top of the stove if not), and the lamb coming free of the bone.

Serve with *chilau* rice (see page 39) or flatbread (page 109).

Autumn pudding

FOR 4 PEOPLE

This is a variation on the classic summer pudding, using the darker fruits of September.

500g apples, a mixture of sweet eaters and sharp cookers
500g mixed blackberries, elderberries, stoned damsons or plums
muscovado sugar, or dark honey
ground cumin (optional)
6 slices of wholemeal bread

Core the apples, but don't peel them, and mix them with the rest of the fruit. The precise proportions aren't really important; regard this pudding as a kind of seasonal fruit stock-pot.

Cook the fruit as it stands, without any extra water, for 15 minutes, until soft. Stir in muscovado sugar or dark honey to taste, and perhaps a pinch of ground cumin seed, as recommended by the French writer Gisèle Tronche in her wild fruit, '*humeur noire*' jam recipes.

Transfer the pulp to a pudding basin lined with slices of whole-meal bread, putting more slices on top to cover the fruit. Put a saucer on top of these last slices, and press it down with a weight of some kind (half a brick is sufficient). Leave in the refrigerator overnight, but take out half an hour before serving

Bullace compote

Made with yellow bullaces, this is so zesty, and such a fresh orange colour, it could almost be a marmalade.

500g yellow bullaces
1 lemon
500g sugar

Stone the bullaces, and stew in just enough water to cover them until they begin to soften, but haven't entirely lost their shape. Add the juice of 1 lemon (this is for flavour, not pectin, which bullaces have plenty of) and the sugar.

Continue to cook until the mixture reaches what's called a 'rolling boil', which means a bubbling activity that can't be stopped by stirring. Begin testing the jam for setting at this point, by removing a very small quantity with a wooden spoon and dripping it on to a *cold* plate (put it in the fridge first, if possible). The jam is at the setting point when the surface of this spot will just wrinkle when pushed with a finger (on a thermometer the setting point is 104°C).

Leave to cool for about 15 minutes, then pour into warm, sterilised jars and seal with standard jam pot covers.

A few odd fruits

Warm wild strawberries on almond paste

THIS IS MORE STRICTLY a summer dish, and was inspired by a patch of wild strawberries growing on a bare limestone slab in the Yorkshire Dales, one baking summer's afternoon. They'd been turned to melting beads of fragrant juice by the heat reflected off the stone, and they merged in my head with a false memory, a Tudor recipe I believed I'd once read for almond biscuits baked in the sun. I suspect now it was fanciful. Things may dry out in sunshine, but they won't bake. Nonetheless it's a nice conceit to have sunning itself on a stone while you eat a summer lunch.

2 tablespoons ground almonds
1 tablespoon caster sugar
milk
a handful of wild strawberries

Mix the almonds and sugar in a bowl, and add milk literally drop by drop, stirring first with a spoon and then with your fingers, until you have a stiff paste. Squeeze this into small thin oblongs, about 4cm long and 3mm thick, top with a few wild strawberries, and leave in full sun on a patio stone or a metal tray. In a couple of hours the strawberries will be warm and squidgy, and the almond paste should have stiffened.

Wild service berry snacks

The revival of interest in this scarce native tree in the 1980s – and a good deal of subsequent planting in nature reserves and parks – means that there are probably more service trees about than at any time since the bad days of woodland clearance in the 1960s. They are handsome trees, covered with umbels of white flowers in May. The bunches of fruits – clusters of round or oval berries a little like large brown haws – appear in late summer. They're hard and bitter at first, but as the autumn progresses, and night frosts begin (or alternatively if they are picked and taken indoors), they begin to 'blet', a process

of ripening in which they become soft and sweet, and
take on a unique taste, with hints of tamarind and
sultana and over-ripe apricot.

Service trees are on the northern edge of
their range in Britain, and are commonest in the
Kent and Sussex Weald. Here they're known as
chequer trees, and the berries as chequers or checkers.
It seemed an inscrutable name, until the botanist Patrick
Roper discovered a curious correlation: several of the many Chequers
pubs in the Weald had service trees growing in their gardens, and
records of the fruits being used to make wine, or a kind of ratafia (see
page 161) with brandy. It seems possible that the berries were back-
named from being used in this way in pubs which were already called
Chequers. (Chequer-boards were often used as generic signs by
pubs, as brass balls are outside pawnbrokers.)

The berries were more straightforwardly eaten as sweets by
children, well into the twentieth century, as a contributor to *Flora
Britannica* remembered: 'I was born in St Michaels near Tenterden,
Kent, and well remember gathering the berries from the tree which
grew in the hedge bordering our garden. They were picked in
clusters and threaded on lengths of string, layer upon layer, which
were then hung in the larder to ripen. We were then allowed to
pick them singly, as they ripened, leaving the strings.' This custom is
being revived here and there, with grown-ups too enjoying the
berries, especially with a glass of whisky.

A pear, lemon and olive salad for cold lamb or mutton

FOR 2 PEOPLE

I thought it might be interesting to make a salad by mixing several of the fruits that go well with lamb, so I put together pears, half-preserved lemons and olives. I used our local Norfolk pears Little Robins, crisp, sharp and rosy-cheeked, which I'd discovered on a feral hedgebank tree. Use your own local variety of dessert pear if possible.

2 small lemons
500g eating pears
20 black Kalamata olives
extra virgin olive oil
white wine vinegar
salt
sugar
fresh rosemary

Five hours before you wish to serve this salad, prepare the lemons. Slice off the tops and tails and cut each lemon into thin segments lengthways. Scrape out as many of the pips as you can see. Then quick-pickle the slices according to the recipe on page 80 – blanch them in boiling water for a minute, cover with salt, sugar and warm vinegar, and press under a weighted plate for 4 to 5 hours.

Just before serving, peel and quarter the pears, cutting away the pithier parts of the core. Stone the olives (as many as you fancy), and mix them with the pears and the drained and rinsed lemon segments.

Make a dressing with roughly equal quantites of olive oil and white wine vinegar, salt, a teaspoon of sugar, and a small sprig of rosemary which has been crushed in a mortar.

Membrillo

Quinces are one of the most beautifully scented of all fruits, and crop increasingly well in the changing British climate. They are beautifully scented, and I always put a quince in the car in autumn, as a natural perfume. But they are barely used in cooking except as an occasional addition to jellies or apple pies. Try them in tagines, with chicken or lamb (page 151). Or make the classic Spanish quince 'cheese' known as *membrillo*, which is served as an accompaniment to meat, hot and cold, and as a filling for tarts.

1kg quinces
sugar
lemon juice

Cut up the quinces roughly (don't bother to peel or core), cover them with water in a large saucepan and bring to the boil. Simmer until they're soft, drain off any excess water, and mash the flesh, either with a potato masher or in a food processor. Then push the mash through a sieve to take out any pips and hard pieces of core. Weigh the resulting purée, add an equal amount of sugar, and put into a saucepan over a low heat. Let it bubble slowly for some while, stirring frequently, until the colour takes on a deep reddish hue, and the purée is quite thick. Taste, and add a squeeze of lemon juice if it's too sweet. Pour on to a tray lined with greaseproof paper, and allow to set. Cut into slices about 2 cm wide and store in sterilised jars.

PS: Fruit cheeses can be made from most hard autumn fruit – apples, damsons, pears – by the same process.

Drinks

THE BASIC PROCESS behind the making of that European-wide favourite sloe gin – soak ripe fruit plus a little sugar in alcohol for a couple of months – can be repeated for just about every fruit. What happens chemically is osmosis, an exchange of fruiting-body fluids. The alcohol draws out the water and soluble flavourings in the fruit through the semi-permeable membrane of its skin and flesh until there is an even concentration throughout the mixture.

Making these flavoured liqueurs is a passion in many parts of Europe. In Denmark they steep herbs as well as berries in aquavit to make aromatic and acerbic *schnapps*. In France – especially in the wine-growing areas – there is still a tradition of making *ratafias* by steeping fruit in home-distilled *eau de vie*.

Here is a generic recipe, using pears as an example.

Pear liqueur

dessert pears (cooking pears can be used, but it is advisable
to cook them a little in a dash of water first)
sugar
vodka

Chop the pears roughly, but don't peel or core. Pack into an airtight
jar or wide-necked bottle (a 2 litre Kilner jar is ideal) so that it is
about two-thirds full. Add 2 to 4 tablespoons of sugar, depending
on how sweet you like your liqueurs. Pour in an entire bottle of
vodka (750ml). Seal and leave for at least 2 months (the longer the
better), turning the jar upside down from time to time to help the
ingredients mix.

When it's ready, strain into bottles though a fine sieve or a piece
of muslin in a funnel.

PS: A canny French trick for making pear liqueur is to slide a bottle
over a just-formed pear while it is still on the tree, taping it to a
branch if necessary. (The bottle-neck is packed with paper to prevent
insects getting in.) The pear grows and ripens in its miniature hot-
house. When ripe – by which time it's beginning to touch the sides
of the bottle – it's broken from the stem, and *eau de vie* and sugar
syrup are poured on top. The result is a Christmas wonder.

Good combinations of fruit and liqueurs

Redcurrants and gin

Blackberries and vodka

Damsons and vodka

Cherries and brandy

Wild-service berries and malt whisky

Apples and brandy

Juniper berries and gin (a double juniper, as it were)

Quince and brandy

Grapes and *marc* (in the Loire this is the only drink

recognised as the true *ratafia*)

Green walnuts and brandy

Vin de cerise

Between 1987 and 1997, I spent a spent a week or so every summer camping with friends in the limestone *causse* country of the south-western Cevennes, an elysium of eagle-haunted gorges and wild orchid pastures. The local food was every bit as botanically rich, and indigenous to a fault. At one restaurant, run by an expatriate Welsh couple who did elaborate consultations with their customers before deciding the menu, we were once served a lime-blossom sorbet made from the actual lime tree under which we'd camped the night before.

My favourite haunt was – and still is – Le Papillon in St Jean du Bruel, which in season serves wild asparagus, mushrooms from the hill pastures, honey made by bees foraging on the *causse* herbs. The restaurant produces its own tangy aperitifs, too, from gentian, walnut, cherries. If they've got enough in store, they sometimes let me buy a bottle to take home – the gaspingly bitter, teak-brown *gentiane* especially, which there's no chance of buying in Britain. But on a whim a couple of autumns ago, I wondered if it might be possible to make the cherry aperitif, their *vin de cerise*, ourselves, and wrote to Madame Papillon to see if she would be prepared to share her house recipe. She replied in exquisite French longhand, and made it clear just what a committed domestic economy she ran. 'When you're making your cherry jam,' she insisted, 'make sure to save all the cherry stones.'

I give the recipe itself in Madame's euphonious French, 'pour 5 litres de vin rouge':

'1kg de sucre
½ litre d'alcool
2 grosses foigues de noix concassés
100 feuilles de cerisier ramasses a l'automne
lorsqu'elles commencent a jaunir
Laisser macérer au moins 40 jours . . .'

A cherry liqueur that does not include any cherries, but two handfuls of crushed stones and a flurry of dying leaves. A ritual maceration for 40 days . . . when I read the letter out to our Francophile friend Nick Wheeler, he said 'That's not a recipe, it's a spell'.

But the spell worked. I did it at one third the quantity, and with some Anglo-Saxon adjustments. We methodically spat out and saved all our cherry stones for a whole summer, fastidiously cleaning them, drying them on a plate, and storing them in an airtight jar. I had to presume the size of Madame Papillon's extremely proficient hands, and guessed a fistful to be about one generous teacup. So in October I measured out this quantity of stones, put them in a tea-cloth and smashed them to bits with a hammer. I also doubled the alcohol volume using vodka, on the assumption that rough French *eau de vie* is stronger. As for the leaves, well, that year our wild cherry trees turned straight from green to vermilion with barely a day or two's yellow in between, and compromises had to be made. If I'd known what the leaves were for, I might have been more discriminating. They seem odourless, and with not much taste beyond that of stringy cellulose. The yellows and reds of autumn are due to anti-oxidants, which protect the leaves while they're transferring their sugars back into the trunk before falling. Maybe they play some preservative role in the liqueur. But I would have thought that the alcohol would have been more than sufficient for this purpose. I decided Nick was probably right, that the whole process was magical, and included some cherry-red leaves to stand in for the absent fruit.

So into a large kilner jar went 1½ litres (2 bottles) of red wine, 330g of sugar, 1 medium fistful of crushed stones, 350cc of vodka, and 30 miscellaneous red and yellowing cherry leaves. About 50 days later (Christmas Eve), I strained the contents into two clean wine bottles.

The resulting dark liquor, ruby tinged with brown as in a hefty Barolo, was eye-wateringly good. The almond aspect of the classic cherry taste (from the stones) had come through, as well as a voluptuous fruitiness (from who knows where), and the alcohol made it feel more like a liqueur than an aperitif. But I'm not sure any of us could have managed a second glass, and next time I will stick to Madame's wise proportions for the vodka.

Scrumping, gleaning and vegetable road-kill

IN THE SOUTH-WEST of France there's still a lively tradition of *la ceuillette*, the seasonal gathering of wild mushrooms, fruits and greens. This is still a useful economic perk for the less well-off, but nobody would pretend that it's essential for survival. *La ceuillette* seems more of a re-enactment of ancient rights over the land, a snub to the notion of nature as private property, a celebration of belonging to one's *pays*.

There's no longer any such deep-rooted tradition in Britain. We've become more deferential to landownership than any other European nation. For the last two centuries, and especially since the Game Acts and Parliamentary Enclosures, landowners have been squeezing the rights of ordinary people in the countryside. The last decade has seen a small swing back, with new Open Access agreements over land, and a perceptible shift in public opinion. But if you're picking wild fruit you are quite likely to come up against the thorny legal question of ownership. In a nutshell: whom does a hedgerow hazel belong to? The law seems clear if a plant is undeniably wild – a blackberry bush, a field mushroom, an elderflower. Flowers and fruit (but not the roots in the soil, which are the landowner's) belong to no one, and only become property by being, in legal jargon, 'rendered into possession' – that is, picked. It's finders keepers. You might (on private property anyway) get done for trespass or criminal damage, but not for theft. A *planted* crop, on the other hand – a field of peas or an orchard plum-tree – is the property of the planter.

But there is a hazy, equivocal territory between these apparently clear-cut extremes, partly due to the fact that plants are no respecters of fences. A walnut tree, say, growing on the edge of a private garden, may have branches which stray into the public domain by extending over a highway or footpath. If it sheds its nuts on the pavement, common sense suggests they are public property, there for the taking. But what if the nuts overhang the path but haven't fallen yet? Does their continued attachment to a private tree anchor them also in the realm of private property? On many nature reserves and managed commons there are, understandably, by-laws prohibiting the picking of any of the vegetation. But what about deliberately planted species in public spaces? Can you garner rowan berries (great for jellies) from the ornamental shrubs in a town street? Or domesticated apples from the trees that have been considerately set down in the verges of trunk roads? (Municipal prissiness may be just as much a problem here as legality. When I was discussing the idea of community orchards once with a town councillor, his major objection was that 'people might pick the fruit'!)

The law seems ambiguous on these points, but not, alas, on the ethically much clearer case of gleaning. This was an ancient practice – going back as far as Mosaic law – in which local people had the right to gather spilt or unsheafed wheat from the fields after harvest. It was one of the last survivals of the communal use of land which once held sway over much of Europe. In England it lingered here and there until the last years of the nineteenth century, and Flora Thompson gives a graphic account in *Lark Rise to Candleford* (first published in 1939, but recalling life in 1880s Oxfordshire):

> . . . flour for the daily pudding and an occasional plain cake
> could be laid in for the winter without any cash outlay. After
> the harvest had been carried from the fields, the women and
> children swarmed over the stubble picking up the ears of wheat
> the horse-rake had missed. Gleaning, or 'leazing', as it was
> called locally.
>
> Up and down and over and over the stubble they hurried, backs
> bent, eyes on the ground, one hand outstretched to pick up the
> ears, the other resting on the small of the back with the 'handful'
> . . . At the end of the fortnight or three weeks that the leazing
> lasted, the corn would be thrashed out at home and sent to the
> miller, who paid himself for grinding by taking toll of the flour.

In Herefordshire there was a tradition of apple gleaning in the orchards, called 'grippling': 'It consists of leaving a few apples, which are called gripples, on every tree, after the general gathering, for the boys, who go with climbing-poles and bags to collect them.'

As an activity, gleaning for wheat fell into disuse. By the early twentieth century it was no longer cost-effective, even for the poor. And while, to my knowledge, it's never been actually outlawed, it has never been explicitly registered as a right either. Perhaps it's now legally regarded as on a par with horse-stealing. A plea of 'customary practice' might be a defence in law, but you would have to prove long continuity.

Which is a shame, because mechanised harvesting generates huge waste in many more crops than wheat. Carrots and onions, for example. We glean onions round the edges of fields in Norfolk where they've been left behind or damaged by the harvesting machines. Once this almost got me my day in court to defend the ancient right. We were scrambling out of a harvested onion-field one evening with a conspicuously bulging bag, to be met by two policemen, in an unmarked car parked next to ours. But they were only concerned that we hadn't broken down, bless them. I'd like to see a restoration of the right of gleaning for vegetable crops, limited (as it always was for grain crops) to a short, fixed period *after* harvest.

Tourrin à l'edredon

I should have used those onions for a dish I only discovered later –
tourrin à l'edredon – otherwise known as eiderdown soup. This is a
thickish onion soup. Traditionally it was made in sufficient quantities
for two meals. After lunch, the tureen was put to bed, under the
eiderdown, to keep warm for a quick reheating before supper. With
gleaned onions, they should also be hidden in the bed *before* cooking.

1kg onions

2 cloves of garlic

olive oil

1 teaspoon sugar

1 tablespoon flour

1 litre water

1 large glass white wine

salt and pepper

optionals: celery, potatoes, tinned tomatoes, ham or bacon

2 egg yolks

In a large, covered saucepan, gently cook the finely sliced onions and
chopped garlic in 3 or 4 tablespoons of olive oil, until they are golden.
This will take about 20 to 30 minutes. Stir in the sugar, flour, water,
wine and seasoning, and add any of the optional extras you fancy

(thinly sliced celery and potatoes, chopped tomatoes, bacon). Bring to the boil and simmer for half an hour. Beat the egg yolks in a bowl and gradually beat in 6 tablespoons of the hot soup. Take the soup off the heat, and stir this mixture in. (But don't boil if you reheat, as it will curdle.) Serve immediately. Traditionally the soup was ladled into bowls containing a slice of bread, with a sprinkle of grated cheese on the top.

Then put the remainder to bed till the evening.

Winter

Fleshy roots, obstinate meat, cold bodies. Winter demands more
energy to cook and more to stay warm. The secret of responsible
winter cooking is to meet both goals in one process. Hot food
means a hot room. Eat in the kitchen if you don't already. Make the
heat you do use do as much work as possible. This is the time of the
stock-pot on the wood-burner, and the stew on the lap.

*

The stock-pot

NOT LONG AGO I watched a group of housewives talking on
television about how they eked out their food budgets.
When asked if they ever considered making soup with the
bones from their roast chickens, they let out a collective howl of
disgust, and made it clear that the interviewer had suggested something
far worse than grave-robbing, and possibly in the realms of necrophilia.
'Dead birds' skeletons? You expect us to *eat* that?' And this from people
who only minutes before had expressed their fondness for off-the-shelf
foods made from the substance euphemistically entitled – a *hommage* to
technological recycling – 'Mechanically Reclaimed Meat Products'.

A stock-pot – by which I mean a rough and ready ongoing soup, to which new ingredients and liquids are added each day, or as they become available, is one of the greatest contributions you can make to reducing food waste. In our house it's carbon squeaky – a way, you might say, of bypassing the compost heap and its globally warming effluvia, and conjuring new foods directly from old. It's also (from daily boiling) free from the dangers of more casually lingering left-overs. But mostly it's an adventure, since you never know exactly what it's going to taste like on any given day.

There is an unnecessary mystique about making soup. In snootier cookbooks, the phrase 'good stock' hovers like a mantra, unexplained and unqualified, as if the rendering of the pure essence of bone or vegetable was a kind of masonic secret, to be neither revealed nor compromised. In my experience almost anything once living will make interesting (if not necessarily 'good') stock if boiled for long enough.

More realistically, utilitarian stock can be made from the simple boiling of a chicken carcass, lamb bones or a ham hock. Trim off any remaining fat from the bones, place in a large saucepan with a couple of chopped onions and carrots, and add water to a level of about 10 to 15cm from the bottom of the pan. Don't attempt to cover the bones with water. Bring to the boil, place the lid of the saucepan on securely, and simmer for about 1½ to 2 hours, pressing the bones down into the broth occasionally as they become loosened from each other. Leave to cool a little, then strain the contents of the pan through a firm sieve into a bowl or second saucepan, pressing as much as you can from the moist residue with a wooden spoon. Leave to become entirely cold, and then, with a small ladle, remove as much you can of the fatty layer which will have risen to the top (or use a siphon if the fat is still liquid).

A pile of remnant vegetables – onions, carrots, potatoes, butternut squash, celery – will make a stock through the same process (or a soup in 10 minutes, if you use a pressure cooker and liquidise the result). Don't rule anything out. Discarded pea-pods will make stock by themselves; onion skins and root peelings give colour and warmth, beans and peas body. Even stale bread makes soup in parts of the Mediterranean. Always use a minimum of water to start with, and add more towards the end of the cooking to achieve the kind of consistency you prefer.

But to build a more complex, ongoing stock, a narrative soup, the plot needs four basic themes:

THE BASE An intensely-flavoured starter such as the gravy from a roast joint, the remains of a casserole or stew, some leftover *al dente* vegetables, a good pile of cooked beans.

THE LIQUID Stock from bones or vegetables (see above), water from cooking potatoes, spinach, onions or beans again. Unfinished bottles of wine.

THICKENERS (optional – you may prefer a thin soup). For their starch: chopped potatoes, cooked or raw; carrots, crushed occasionally as the soup simmers; a handful of pearl barley, rice, bread-crumbs, porridge oats or lentils.

FLAVOURINGS AND SHARPENERS A soup with an accumulating cargo of vegetables and slowly disintegrating meat can become, shall we say, a tad full-bodied. It may need lightening or sharpening. The juice of a lemon will help cut fattiness. A dash of soy sauce or dry sherry adds depth. A pinch of chilli powder cures most ills. Keep testing and adding till the blend pleases you.

There are almost no taboos in developing a stock-pot, though you should use your common sense. A few scraps of sharp fruit – apple, orange – can do marvels with a meat-based stock, though bananas are an acquired taste. Even fish and meat can occasionally meet in a soup, as in the chowderish combination of bacon and the milk in which a smoked haddock has been cooked.

This is the track taken by one week's stock. It began with the sauce and a few portions of meat from a successful though over-generous beef vindaloo. It was augmented on succeeding days by the water from a dish of quick-boiled spinach, then the more orthodox stock from a stewed chicken, finally with remains of a vegetable risotto. Each day it was boiled for about a quarter of an hour. Then on day five the contents of the saucepan were liquidised, and produced a broth with the character of Mediterranean mulligatawny.

To liquidise or not is a matter of choice. I quite often leave the morsels of vegetable and meat to float around to provide a variety of texture, or use a potato masher rather than an electric blender to leave the soup more grainy.

Stock-pots can theoretically go on indefinitely, provided you go through the discipline of boiling them for at least 15 minutes each day – or more, if you're adding new solid ingredients. But I reckon a week is the preferable maximum, after which all stocks converge towards an homogeneous brown gruel, and staleness begins to be a possibility. Before that, every day should generate a *potage surprise*.

But we have favourite special winter soups, that are made to more formal recipes:

Ploughman's lunch soup
FOR 4 PEOPLE

The inspiration for this came from a Cheddar cheese, brown bread and apple soup devised by William Bavin at our local restaurant, Weavers, in Diss, and served with 'Branston crème fraîche'. William excels at culinary puns, and I don't think he will object to the slight extensions I've made to his original idea, extending the Ploughman's Lunch motif by adding a few grapes for sweetness and onions for bite, and putting some of the beer which traditionally accompanies the dish *into* the soup.

2 crisp eating apples
2 medium red onions
2 slices of wholemeal bread
about 15 seedless white grapes
half a pint bitter ale
1 tablespoon malt vinegar
125g mature Cheddar
salt and pepper
2 to 3 tablespoons crème fraîche
1 tablespoon Branston, or similar dark pickle

Peel and core the apples, quarter the onions, trim the crusts off the bread, and put into a saucepan with the grapes and 285ml water. Bring to the boil, and simmer for 10 minutes, until the apples have softened. Liquidise. Add the beer, the vinegar, the cheese, grated, and salt and pepper to taste. Reheat, stirring well until the cheese is melted. Then serve, and on to each plateful float a stirred (but not blended) mixture of crème fraîche and pickle.

Ribollita
FOR 4 PEOPLE

The name means simply 'reboiled', and in Italy *ribollita* covers many diverse *mélanges* of vegetables, beans and bread. The 'black kale' Cavalo nero is always included in the most characteristic versions, but if you can't find this, curly kale or Savoy cabbage will do.

2 medium onions

carrots (at least 250g)

4 cloves of garlic

a head of celery

extra virgin olive oil

parsley

fennel seeds (optional)

dark green cabbage leaves – up to 500g

a small tin of plum tomatoes

100g fresh beans, from runner bean pods (see pages 100–101),
or previously cooked haricot or Borlotti beans

4 slices of bread (Italians would use *ciabatta*)

water or stock

Peel the onions, scrape the carrots, crush and peel the garlic, trim the celery of leaf and dark streaks, and roughly chop the whole lot. Stew gently in a good splash of olive oil in a large saucepan for about half an hour. Add chopped parsley and, if you like, ½ a teaspoon of fennel seeds. Destalk the cavalo nero or cabbage, tear into small pieces, and add, together with the tomatoes and beans. Stew for 30 minutes, then season and add the bread (chopped or broken into small pieces).

Ribollita should be thick but not solid, and this is the time to start adding water or stock (vegetable or chicken) – stirring quite frequently so that the bread starts to soften and break up. Dilute gradually and simmer for another 15 minutes, until the consistency is right for you. It should be velvety from the dissolved starch from the beans and bread. Serve with a gout of olive oil on the surface of each plateful. (Or maybe a dipping dish of olive oil on the side. Polly's Scottish dad had a special oval cream-dipping dish for his porridge, through which each spoonful of the oats was drawn before eating.)

Turnip soup
FOR 2 PEOPLE

We were served this one night in a lonely restaurant in the Auvergne. The meal was full of local specialities, including the region's star dish, *chou farci,* cabbage stuffed with local sausage. But it was the turnip soup, *soupe aux navets*, that was the star that evening. It was mellow, smooth, subtly aromatic. We asked the rather shy local girl who was serving us how it was made, and she became animated by our intimation that a hefty dose of cream must have been used. 'Pas de crème,' she insisted. And cream did indeed prove quite superfluous when Polly began experimenting with our own turnips.

It's the incongruity of this soup's luxuriance that makes it such a wonderful surprise. Turnips are regarded as little better than animal fodder in Britain, and rarely make an appearance in either restaurants or cookbooks. Jane Grigson remarked that 'We stick too much to the agricultural view, regarding the turnip as a coarse, cow-sized vegetable, suitable for the overwintering of herds, schoolchildren, prisoners and lodgers.'

But even the herds are getting high-quality turnips now, and a useful source of free roots are the ones that fall off the back of tractors on the way to the fields in the morning.

500g turnips
butter
500ml vegetable stock or water
salt and pepper

Peel and chop the turnips and fry gently in butter for 10 minutes or so, until they have just begun to soften. Add the stock or water, bring to the boil, and simmer for half an hour. Allow to cool a little, then liquidise until very smooth (a minute at least). Add salt and pepper, and more water if it's too thick for you.

You can of course include cream if you want a richer soup, or mix potatoes with the turnips for a thicker one. But the taste of turnip is so exceptional that you may prefer it with the minimum of diversions.

The pig's squeal

IF HAPLESS ANIMALS — expensively reared, greenhouse-gas-producing animals — are to continue to be a major part of our diet, then I think we owe it to them and to the planet to waste as little of them as possible. Use everything but the squeal, as was proverbially said of the country pig. Dorothy Hartley gives a roll call of honour of the uses of pig bits at the time when every cottager kept one. It's a lesson in frugal housekeeping, and a footnote on the origins of some modern snacks.

> Practically nothing is wasted in a good pig. The head might be cooked as a 'boar's head' dish, but more likely the cheeks were made into 'Bath chaps'. The gristly ears, head, bone and tail are at once put down to make the strong jelly stock. The soft meat — that is the pig's fry, kidneys and liver — were eaten at once. If the first consideration was bacon, the fore-legs were cut with the sides for bacon, and the hind legs only for ham . . . All trimmings of the meat were chopped into a basin which had been rubbed with onions. The meat was then scattered with chopped sage and black pepper ready for pork pie. The flead was set in an iron pot on the stove for lard. The trotters and tripe were usually cooked with onions and white sauce, and the extracted bones from the trotters were added to the head and

trimmings already simmering, to be made into brawns. Black puddings had been made by the butcher with barley, oats and rice. When no more lard could be squeezed from the scraps in the iron pot, they were 'fried to a finish', and the crisp brown pieces called 'scratchings' were sprinkled with freshly chopped parsley and a dash of vinegar.

We ate a lot of offal when I was a child. My father worked in the City, close to Smithfield meat market, and brought home animal organs with the same collector's glee as he did bits from the insides of war-surplus electronic gear. Not all of it was welcome. Tripe continues to be one of the few foods I find hard to eat. My hapless mother had

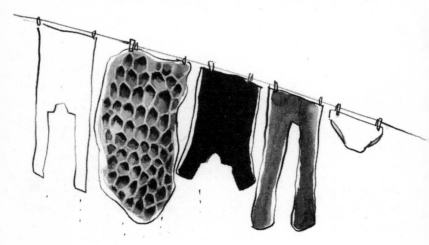

to cauterise sheets of it in a big aluminium boiler – the same one, I swear, that she used for the washing. Certainly the stale, soapy smell was the same, and hung about the house for days.

But oxtails, stuffed hearts, and best of all lamb's sweetbreads – hard to obtain in retail butchers these days – became lasting favourites. Many have gone out of fashion in these squeamish times, and in consequence have become some of the cheapest and best-value cuts of meat, and among the few with which you can feed two people for under a pound.

Oxtail stew
FOR 2 PEOPLE

Oxtail stew was a traditional Saturday dish in our family, especially during the rugby season, when I was allowed to eat it on my lap in front of the television. It was one of those comforting rituals which made winter bearable: a pint with friends beforehand, the ebbing and flowing stew perched precariously on a tray, the mandatory pile of butter beans on the side, and always one's attention on the action on the screen, so that the dish had to win by its inner warmth and tactile jelliness. Sucking the gelatinous discs off the end of each vertebra was the very best part of the meal.

1 oxtail (about 8 pieces)

plain flour

sunflower oil

4 carrots

2 sticks of celery

2 large onions

1 glass of red wine

a bunch of fresh thyme

Worcestershire sauce

200g butter beans (reconstituted dried ones if possible,

but tinned if not)

juice of 1 lemon

salt and pepper

It's best if you can prepare this stew a day in advance. The flavour's better, and it gives you the chance to ladle off some of the plenteous fat that oxtails release.

Carve off as much of the yellow exterior fat as you can from the oxtail pieces. Roll them in seasoned flour, and fry them in a couple of tablespoons of oil in a heavy-bottomed saucepan or big casserole dish until they're brown on all sides. Remove from the pan.

Wash the carrots and celery and slice them into 2cm wide chunks. Peel and slice the onions similarly and brown them in the same pan, adding a dash more oil if necessary. Put the oxtail back into the pan, add the wine, thyme, a good dash of Worcestershire sauce, and enough water to cover the lot. Bring to the boil and simmer gently for 3 hours. Then remove the pieces of meat and vegetable to a dish with a slotted spoon. Leave the liquid to stand overnight in the saucepan.

The next day, skim off the fat which will have risen to the surface and partly solidified. Return the meat and vegetables to the pan. Add the butter beans now, if they have been reconstituted (if tinned, add 10 minutes befrore the end). Add the lemon juice and season as desired. Simmer on top of the stove for a further 1 to 2 hours, or, if you are using a casserole dish, in a preheated oven at 150°C/gas 2.

Serve with a large napkin.

Liver chop suey
FOR 2 PEOPLE

The kind of chop suey served in Western restaurants is probably a Western invention. The name literally means 'food scraps' or bits and pieces, and one story suggests that the dish was invented as a black joke by a Chinese statesman visiting England in the 1890s. But there are, of course, recipes for leftovers in Chinese cuisine, and this is based on one from Singapore. I've adapted it to use largely British vegetables, but you can add or substitute Chinese ingredients at will. Don't be put off by the thought of prawns and liver in the same dish: it works. Regard it as an Oriental 'Turf and Surf'.

French beans
1 medium onion
2 cloves of garlic
1 red pepper
1 carrot
50g button mushrooms
1 red chilli
Savoy cabbage
sunflower oil
50g cooked pork
50g pig's or lamb's liver
125g prawns

For the sauce
1 dessertspoon cornflour
1 tablespoon water
1 tablespoon sunflower oil
1 tablespoon soy sauce
1 tablespoon oyster sauce
1 tablespoon dry sherry

Top and tail the beans. Chop the onion roughly. Peel and crush the garlic. Quarter the red pepper and remove its core, and, along with all the other vegetables, slice into thin (0.5 to 1cm wide) strips. Make a dash of sunflower oil very hot in a wok, and stir-fry all the vegetables (see page 78) for 3 minutes. Do them separately if you have the patience. Remove from the wok and set aside.

Slice the pork into 2cm wide strips and fry in a little fresh oil. Slice the liver as thinly as you can, and fry that too – 2 minutes each for both meats.

Make the sauce by mixing all the ingredients together, taking care to stir out any lumps in the cornflour. Return all the ingredients to the wok, add the prawns and sauce, and heat briefly, stirring and mixing well, until the sauce just starts to thicken.

Serve with plain boiled rice (pages 38–9).

Creamy chicken liver pâté
FOR 4 PEOPLE

1 small onion
1 clove of garlic
250g chicken livers
fresh thyme
1 small glass of brandy
20g butter
salt and pepper
optional: 15g gelatine, 60ml double cream, 2 egg whites

Slice the onion, garlic and livers roughly, add a spoonful or so of thyme leaves, and fry for about 10 minutes. Allow to cool a little, add the brandy, salt and pepper, and transfer to a food processor. Blend for about 2 minutes. If you want an even creamier finish, transfer to the liquidiser for a final whirl, then put on a plate and refrigerate.

Alternatively, dissolve the gelatine in 100ml of water, and stir this liquid together with the cream into the processed livers. Wait for a while until the mixture starts to set, then fold in the whisked egg whites. This is more strictly a mousse, so spoon into a mould or pâté dish, and refrigerate.

Elena's mustard kidneys
FOR 2 PEOPLE

All of us who began to discover continental food in Soho in the last decades of the twentieth century are indebted to Elena Salvoni. As *maîtresse d'* in a string of legendary West End restaurants – the Café Bleu in the 1940s, then Bianchi's, L'Escargot, the Gay Hussar, and finally L'Étoile (now Elena's L'Étoile) – she has patiently interpreted the mysteries of European cuisine to three generations of nervous *ingénus*. Stephen Fry calls Elena 'his other mother'.

This is L'Étoile's way with devilled kidneys, adapted a little for home eating. Elena dedicates the recipe, unnervingly, to Sir Richard Attenborough.

1 shallot
butter
3 tablespoons white wine
100ml double cream
1 tablespoon wholegrain mustard
salt and pepper
400g lamb kidneys

To make the sauce, cut the shallot fine, and simmer in just a spoonful of butter until transparent. Add the wine and simmer for a few minutes until the liquid is reduced by about a third of its original volume. Stir in the cream, and the mustard, and salt and pepper as required. Put to one side.

Slice the kidneys lengthways, and remove the tangle of tubes and gristle at the centre with the point of a sharp knife. Melt a knob of butter in another pan, and sear the kidneys in it for about 5 minutes, until they are browned on all sides. Add the mustard sauce, bring to the boil and serve.

Stuffed heart

FOR 2 PEOPLE

Sympathetic magic works with hearts. Being almost pure muscle, they are as healthy for your own pump as venison, and have one of the smoothest, firmest textures of any meat. A traditional sage and onion stuffing is all they need.

4 lamb's hearts

4 large onions

a handful of sage leaves

250g breadcrumbs

1 egg

salt and pepper

water or stock

Put the peeled and roughly chopped onions, sage leaves, bread-crumbs, egg, salt and pepper into a blender. Whizz briefly, adding water or stock until you have a firm paste.

Trim any fat from the outside of the hearts, and remove the venticles and any arterial tubes with the end of a thin, sharp knife. Press the stuffing into the hearts. Mum used to pinch the open tops together with small skewers, but this isn't necessary if you pack them close together in a small, greased baking pan.

Roast in a preheated oven at 180°C/gas 4 for 45 minutes, turning once – or for less time, if you prefer your meat on the rare side.

Power-saving cookery

BACK IN THE 1970s I worked for *Vole*, an eccentric and unclassifiable magazine started by the late Richard Boston, part a green *Private Eye*, part a satirical *TLS*. Alas, it was three decades ahead of its time (nobody seems to have the *cojones* – CO Jones was Boston's by-line in the magazine – to crack eco-humour now), and it folded after four glorious years.

The most famous edition was the Slow Issue, dedicated to everything from slow food to slow trains. In it was a recipe for the Slow Egg, which required wrapping an egg in black paper and leaving it in very hot sun for the best part of day. The egg should hard-boil, though I have to say I've never succeeded in getting beyond a vague white coagulation. It may be hot enough to fry eggs on the sidewalk in some parts of the world, but in Britain sun-cooking is still a fantasy. Sun-drying is another matter, and a prolonged hot spell in the summer will dry out tomatoes on a tray in a few days. Just remember to bring them in at sunset, so that they don't re-absorb water during the night.

Saving energy in cooking is chiefly a matter of making one source of power heat up several things at once. The ashes of a bonfire will cook potatoes in their jackets and – provided the embers are not red-hot – meat wrapped in foil. The top of a wood-burning stove is one of the best places to slow-cook stews and stock-pots (see page 173).

But so is the top of a central-heating unit, if you bring the pan to the boil on a conventional stove first and then find a way of balancing it on the radiator's surface. A friend once successfully ripened some avocados by strapping them to the top of his car radiator for the journey from London to Norfolk.

There is also the more practical idea of cooking several dishes, or courses, inside a single pot or container. One traditional portable lunch for field-workers was called a 'clanger'. It was a pasty with meat at one end and fruit at the other, which was baked and eaten as a single item. At home, in most poor country households, it was customary to cook all the ingredients of a meal in a single pot up until 1920s. The meat, vegetables, suet puddings were each contained in a separate net inside a large pan of simmering water on the fire. I can remember this practice surviving as the 'bargee's pail' on working boats on the Grand Union canal when I was a boy. A tall pot was packed with meat at the bottom, veg in the middle, and finally, separated by a pastry strip, a layer of chopped apple. The pot was covered with a cloth and simmered in a large pail of water, along with a bottle of tea.

In central Spain one winter, I had a one-pot lunch at a remote farm in the cork-oak savannahs of Extremadura, which are known locally as *dehesas*. Our hosts ran a post-modern, self-sufficient ranch, raising sheep and goats and the local dark brown pigs — *cerdos ibéricos,* close relatives of wild boar. They harvested acorns for the pigs, cork from the cork-oaks, branches for turning into charcoal for the north European barbecue market. They grew their own corn and vegetables. They sent their children to university and had satellite dishes for their generator-powered TV.

We crammed into the tiny kitchen with the whole family. Grandma sat at a table in the corner with the two daughters (not everything is changing in rural Spain), and the entire meal was contained in a huge cauldron, which had been cooked in the kitchen's open hearth. First the liquid was ladled out, as a soup. It was quite thin, but well flavoured with ham and chickpeas. Then came the chickpeas themselves, served as a vegetable course. Finally, lurking at the bottom of the pot, was the *entrée*: cryptic lumps of ham and wickedly gelatinous slabs of garlicky fat.

Pumpkin stew, cooked in its own shell
FOR 4 PEOPLE

In her feisty account of a year growing and living off her own produce, *Animal, Vegetable, Miracle*, the writer Barbara Kingsolver takes some splendid swipes at American fast-food culture. She's appalled by a nation where pumpkins are sprawling in every other open lot and all the recipes say 'take 1 can pumpkin'. On her imaginary shopping list she adds: take '"1 of those big orangey things from the doorstep" . . . Come *on* people. Doesn't anyone remember how to take a big old knife, whack open a pumpkin, scrape out the seeds and bake it? We can carve a face on to it, but can't draw and quarter it. Are we not a nation known worldwide for our cultural zest for blowing up flesh, on movie and video screen and/or armed conflict? Are we in actual fact too squeamish to stab a large knife into a pumpkin? Wait till our enemies find out.'

She's determined not just to cook a real pumpkin, but to make a show of it, cooking a soup inside the shell, as a kind of vegetable tureen. Everyone thought that it would 'taste exactly the same if we just smashed it up'. But Barbara wanted 'some kind of large, autumn-nally harvested *being*, not just ingredients, as the centrepiece of our meal'. She eventually performs something close to 'trephination' on a monster Queensland Blue, and creates 'a battle-weary but still reasonably presentable hollowed-out tureen'.

This is my own version, jigged up a little by ideas from that Spanish cauldron.

1 large pumpkin
plenty of chicken or vegetable stock
2 cloves of garlic
salt and pepper
optional: 500g loin of pork

With a sharp, long-bladed knife cut a circle about 15cm wide round the stalk of the pumpkin. If you can, cut on the slant, so the resulting lid will fit back snugly. Remove the disc and keep.

With a dessertspoon, scoop out as much of the stringy pith and seeds as you can, and discard. Fill the cavity with stock, and add chopped garlic, salt and pepper. (Also add the pork, chopped into bite-sized cubes, if you want a meat dish rather than a simple vegetarian soup.) Replace the lid, putting a single sheet of foil between it and the rest of the pumpkin, to prevent it falling in. Put into a large heatproof bowl – just in case it collapses – and place in an oven at 150°C/gas 2.

After about 45 minutes, take it out of the oven; remove the pumpkin lid, and with a spoon gently scrape the pumpkin flesh from the inside of the shell into the liquid. Replace in the oven and repeat after another 45 minutes. The dish should be cooked in 2 hours.

Serve as soup, plain and simple, or as two or three courses (soup, pumpkin flesh, meat) with the pork pieces at the end.

The Three Shepherds' pie

FOR 4 PEOPLE

This was a shepherd's pie made immediately after Christmas, with the remnants of three seasonal meats, turkey, ham and pork. My apologies to those for whom the terms cottage and shepherd's pies have more precise meanings.

Shepherd's pie is unique to Britain, and is one of our greatest one-pot meals, not so much because it cooks the potatoes (and sometimes other vegetables) with the meat, but because it *steams* them, finishing the carbohydrate in the vapours of the rest of the ingredients, in the manner of Middle Eastern dishes such as *shirini polo* (page 41).

500g potatoes
approx. 1kg leftover ham, pork and turkey or chicken, with a few
carrots or turnips to make up the weight, if necessary
a few tomatoes
2 large onions
1 heaped tablespoon fresh or dried thyme
½ teaspoon crushed fennel seed
sunflower oil

For the gravy
1 level teaspoon curry powder
1 tablespoon tomato purée
dash of Worcestershire sauce
salt and pepper
500ml stock (ham, turkey or vegetable)

Peel the potatoes and boil until they are just mashable, maybe 15 to
20 minutes. Cut the meat (and carrots, etc. if used), tomatoes and
onions into large pieces. Mince roughly in a food processor with the
thyme and fennel seed, but don't make the meat too fine. Fry the lot
in a little oil until the minced onions have turned golden. Put in a
casserole or pie dish.

Make the gravy by stirring the curry powder, tomato purée,
Worcestershire sauce and seasoning into the stock. One of the most
important factors in making a successful shepherd's pie is to add

enough of this mollifying sauce. This is what scents and completes the cooking of the potatoes, bubbles up into its lower layers, and oozes out to produce that prime tit-bit, the sticky, toffee-ish, half-burned alloy of meat and spud (our answer to *dig*, page 40) at the edges of the pot. So add enough for liquid to be visible when you press the top of the meat down with a spoon.

Cover the meat with the mashed potato and smooth it down with a fork so as to produce a very shallow dome. Cook in a preheated oven at about 180°C/gas 4 for 50 minutes, until the top of the potato has begun to brown, and the edges are caramelised.

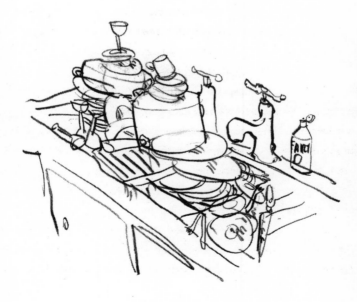

Sechuan aubergine and pork
FOR 2 PEOPLE

This is a one-pot dish for leftover pork and aubergines — a kind of Chinese moussaka, based on a traditional recipe from Sechuan. Its taste is extraordinary, a combination of sweet and sour, hot and salt. It can be made with fresh pork mince, but I prefer cooked meat, which is much less fatty.

2 aubergines

sunflower oil

250g leftover pork

2 cloves of garlic

1 red chilli

1 tablespoon chopped root ginger

2 tablespoons finely chopped spring onions

2 tablespoons soy sauce

2 tablespoons sherry vinegar

2 tablespoons dry sherry

1 tablespoon brown sugar

ground black pepper

salt

sesame oil

100ml stock

Top and tail the aubergines, quarter them lengthways, and then cut across to give roughly 3cm cubes. Heat a wok, add a good gout of sunflower oil, and stir-fry the aubergines for about 5 minutes, until they are soft and slightly browned. Drain, and set aside on a folded sheet of kitchen roll.

Mince the pork in a food processor, but keep it coarse. Chop the garlic and chilli and have ready on a plate with the ginger and spring onions.

Wipe the wok clean. Add another tablespoon of oil and heat well. Stir-fry the pork for about 3 minutes. Add the garlic, chilli, ginger and spring onions, and cook for a further 2 minutes. Then add the aubergines, the rest of the flavourings, a sprinkle of sesame oil, and the stock. Bring to the boil and cook over a high heat until the aubergines are tender and the liquid much reduced. Serve hot or cold.

Fiesta

But the time comes when a feast is called for, when the culinary ducking and diving is used, for once, on sumptuous ingredients. On feast days do something to make the cooking as special as the eating. Sharpen your knives. Put on a clean apron. When my brother David was cooking his epic curries, he used to don a bandana and play Grateful Dead albums as background music (great for the intensity of flavours, not so good for the delivery time).

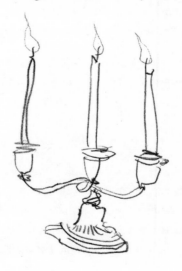

A Valentine's Day Supper

THIS WAS A SUPPER I cooked for Polly. Some of the ingredients are on the lavish side, but each course has a play-off between sharp and sweet, and each uses some of the ideas explored in this book.

Chestnut and apple soup
FOR 2 PEOPLE

This is a winter soup from the south of France, made with the house staple, chestnuts. Prunes can be substituted for the apples.

150g eating apples, russets for preference
500g peeled chestnuts, fresh or vacuum-packed (see pages 116–17)
500ml goat's milk
salt and pepper
50g dark chocolate

Peel, core and roughly chop the apples. Put them into a saucepan with the chestnuts and the milk, and simmer for 40 to 50 minutes, until the chestnuts begin to break up when you prod them. Add more milk, if the blend is too thick for your taste, and seasoning, then liquidise the soup in a food processor. I floated a few snowdrops (thank you, Sarah) on to the served soup, and then some grated bitter chocolate, which Jenny Baker recounts is used as a garnish for this soup in the Ardèche. It seems an odd marriage of peasant and chic, but the result is thrilling, as the wicked, voluptuous bitterness of the chocolate insinuates itself into the homely fruitiness.

Fillet-steak hearts with steak tartare garnish
FOR 2 PEOPLE

I cut the fillet steaks into the shape of hearts. The trimmings were too good to waste, so I made them into little dumplings of highly seasoned steak *tartare*, to serve as a kind of condiment.

2 fillet steaks, each about 300g
fillet steak trimmings (used raw)
1 small onion
1 egg yolk
1 teaspoon capers
2 or 3 gherkins
1 teaspoon Dijon mustard
fresh ground black pepper
dash of Worcestershire sauce
1 teaspoon chopped parsley

Put all the ingredients except the steaks into a food processor, and mince for a few seconds. Taste for balance, and add more mustard, capers, etc. if necessary. Continue to process until the mixture is quite creamy.

Cook the steaks to your liking. I was taught to dress steak with a squeeze of lemon juice by the effusive Vincenzo Iannone, who ran our local *trattoria* in the Chilterns for 25 years.

I served them with fresh salsify in a velouté sauce, and potatoes first parboiled, and then crushed before being roast.

Benjamin Britten's Symphony
FOR 2 PEOPLE

We found this recipe in Polly's mother's handwritten recipe book. It's a dessert jelly of dark and glamorous flavours, in truth more like Ravel in Aspic than something by the composer of the austere *Peter Grimes*. But family legend has it that it was indeed invented by Britten. We asked our friend Ronald Blythe, who knew Ben well, if he'd heard of it. He hadn't, but remembered that both Ben and Peter Pears adored 'nursery food' – which would at least explain the jelly if not the combination of sherry and black treacle, which gives the concoction an almost meaty savour, like a bitter-sweet, alcoholic consommé.

2 sachets gelatine
5 tablespoons black treacle
lemon juice
fino sherry

Melt the gelatine powder in about 400ml of hot water in a measuring jug. Stir well and make sure there is no undissolved sludge at the bottom. Stir in the black treacle until it is thoroughly mixed. Then add the juice of 1 lemon, a schooner of fino sherry, and enough water to make up the liquid to one litre. Let it cool, and allow to solidify in the fridge for not less than 3 hours.

A Wakes feast

THE WAKES is a festival still held in some English parishes on the Patronal day of the parish church, or sometimes, tapping into a more ancient tradition still, at the end of hay-making or harvest. In many places it's been transferred to the summer holiday period. The following recipes are all traditional, and use a lot of fruit.

Mucky-mouth pie
FOR 4 PEOPLE

This bilberry and batter pie can be eaten as a dessert, but like all Yorkshire puds can also precede the main meal. Use wild bilberries (often known locally as wimberries), which fruit in moorland all over the north and west of Britain in August, not the blander American blueberries. The best I have eaten, in north Yorkshire itself, had sprigs of mint among the berries.

4 tablespoons flour

1 egg

1 tablespoon sugar

1 cup of milk

butter

250g bilberries

a handful of fresh mint leaves

Make a batter with the flour, egg, sugar and milk, beating out the lumps before adding much of the milk, and continuing till it has the consistency of double cream. Grease a baking tray with a little butter and pour the batter in. Mix the bilberries and mint leaves and strew them evenly across the batter. Bake in an oven at about 170°C/gas 3 for half an hour.

And remember the pie's name before you look in a mirror after eating it.

Hindle Wakes

FOR 4 PEOPLE

This is a spectacular and very ancient festive dish, a reminder that cooking meat and fruit together was traditional in Britain long before the importing of Middle Eastern recipes. It's basically a chicken stuffed with prunes, coated with lemon sauce and served cold on Wakes night. 'Hindle' is not a place name but a corruption of Hen de la Wake.

500g reconstituted and stoned damson prunes or
bought plum prunes, plus a few for the garnish
2 thick slices of wholemeal bread
a cupful of white wine vinegar
a small glass of brandy
salt and pepper
1 chicken, about 2kg, the older the better
2 tablespoons muscovado sugar
100g butter
2 tablespoons plain flour
3 lemons
milk
parsley

Soak the prunes in water for a few hours, then make up the stuffing by mixing them with the bread, decrusted and roughly torn, about 100ml of the white wine vinegar, the brandy, salt and pepper. Blend in a food processor until the stuffing begins to turn over on itself. Add more vinegar if necessary.

Stuff the chicken firmly with the prune mixture. Tie the legs together, and put into a large deep pan. Add the remainder of the vinegar and the sugar and top up with just enough water to cover the bird. Bring to the boil, put a lid on the pan, and reduce the heat so that the liquid is barely simmering. Leave it on the stove overnight – or if you are reluctant to do this, make sure it gets at least 6 hours' cooking. Allow the bird to cool right down in the liquid (which may be almost set solid as this point), otherwise it may fall apart. Remove to a large plate to drain.

Make a lemon sauce by melting the butter in a saucepan and stirring in the flour until all the lumps have gone. Add the juice of 2 of the lemons (saving the grated rind) and then gradually add milk, warming and stirring all the while, until the sauce has the consistency of double cream.

Spoon the sauce over the chicken. It should be thick enough to solidify almost as you apply it. Use a knife to spread it on to any areas of meat left uncovered. Finally scatter the grated lemon rind over the whole surface, and remove the trussing so that the stuffing is visible and accessible. Garnish the whole dish with parsley, prunes, and the remaining lemon, cut in wedges, and serve with a green salad.

The contrast of the yellow coating and the dark purplish stuffing is as dramatic visually as it is to the taste. Only one traditional dish beats it as a centrepiece, and that is the Cockatrice, in which the back end of a rabbit, sewn on to a chicken (head and neck retained), is similarly stuffed, glazed and served cold with extravagant ornamentation.

Almond and orange cake
FOR 4 PEOPLE

This cake, with wheat flour replaced by ground almonds, originated as a Passover dish among Jewish communities in Spain. Oranges reached the Mediterranean in Roman times, and arrived in Britain in the mid-seventeenth century. Doubtless some form of this cake came not much later, and now it's popular for festive occasions throughout the year.

The recipe below is based on one by Claudia Roden.

2 large oranges

6 eggs

1 teaspoon baking powder

250g ground almonds

250g sugar

Boil the oranges whole for 2 hours, then slice them, remove the pips, and purée in a food processor. Beat the eggs, and blend in the baking powder, almonds and sugar. Mix in the orange pulp, and pour into a greased cake tin about 25cm wide.

Bake in a preheated oven at 180°C/gas 4 for 1 to 1¼ hours, until the cake is firm to tap. Leave to cool before turning out.

Afters word

Bᴜᴛ I ꜰɪɴᴅ I can't banish *Lemon Pond Pudding* (page 15) to the limbo of dietary correctness. The memory of that sweet and gloopy suet concoction we made at scout camp won't go away. It's a variation on the traditional Sussex Pond Pudding, with added lemons.

for the suet crust
350g self-raising flour
175g suet
salt

for the filling
4 lemons
4oz unsalted butter
2oz demerara sugar

Make the suet crust by sifting the flour into a bowl with a pinch of salt. Shred the suet with a coarse grater into the flour. Add a little water and work the mixture into a thick dough with a knife at first, then with your hands. Continue adding and kneading until you have a soft dough. Place it on a floured board and work it with a rolling pin until it is an even 1cm thick. Cut into two pieces and roll into round shapes.

Mix the butter and sugar and pat into a flattish roll. Place this on one of the pastry circles. Remove the peel from the lemons and as much of the pith as you can without dismembering them. Cut the lemons in half, and put on top of the butter and sugar. Gather up the edges of the crust, and enclose the peel-less lemons and butter by draping the other slice of crust over the top, and pinching it securely to the first.

Tie up in a floured cloth , and boil in a large saucepan for 2 hours.

And dream of cooking it out of doors, in a billy-can over a wood fire.

A few more books

OLIVE OIL

Mort Rosenblaum, *Olives. The Life and Lore of a Noble Fruit*, 1996. Good on the diversity of the world's oils, and what global commerce is depriving us of.

IDENTIFICATION GUIDES

Roger Phillips, *Wild Food*, 1983

Marjorie Blamey and Christopher Grey-Wilson, *The Illustrated Flora of Britain and North-western Europe*, 1989

ANCIENT COOKING

Jean Bottero, *The Oldest Cuisine in the World. Cooking in Mesopotamia*, 2004

FRUIT FORESTS AND APPLES

Barrie E. Juniper and David J. Mabberley, *The Story of the Apple*, 2006

Sue Clifford and Angela King, *The Apple Source Book*, 2007

Autumnal stuff not covered in the book

JAMS AND PRESERVES

David and Rose Mabey, *Jams, Pickles and Chutneys*, 1975

MUSHROOMS

Marcel Bon, *The Mushrooms and Toadstools of Britain and North-western Europe*, 1987

Roger Phillips, *Mushrooms and other fungi of Great Britain and Europe*, 1981

Jane Grigson, *The Mushroom Feast*, 1975

Index